Math in Motion

FIRST STEPS IN MUSIC THEORY

ANSWER KEY

Caleb Skogen

Caleb Skogen, *Math in Motion: First Steps in Music Theory, Answer Key*

Published by Classical Conversations® MultiMedia, Inc.
P.O. Box 909
West End, NC 27376
www.ClassicalConversations.com | www.ClassicalConversationsBooks.com

Cover design by Classical Conversations. Cover image: *Music and Literature*, William Michael Harnett, 1878. Courtesy of the Albright-Knox Art Gallery, public domain.

All Scripture quotations, unless otherwise noted, are taken from the King James Version of the Bible.

Printed in the United States of America

ISBN: 978-0-9965660-0-1

Table of Contents

EXERCISE ANSWERS

CHAPTER 1—Music Grammar Part 1: The Keyboard and Notation......5

CHAPTER 2—Music Grammar Part 2: Symbols and Notes......17

CHAPTER 3—Introduction to Rhythm......25

CHAPTER 4—Time Signature and Simple Meter......33

CHAPTER 5—Major and Natural Minor Scales......39

CHAPTER 6—Key Signatures......47

CHAPTER 7—Scale Degrees and Transposing......55

CHAPTER 8—Intervals......65

CHAPTER 9—Triads and Triad Qualities......75

CHAPTER 10—Triads: Roman Numeral Analysis......81

CHAPTER 11—Triad Inversions......89

CHAPTER 12—Score Analysis......97

CHAPTER 13—Review......107

BONUS CHAPTER—Compound Meter......117

SCORE ANALYSES......125

1 Music Grammar Part I: The Keyboard and Notation

Chapter 1 Review

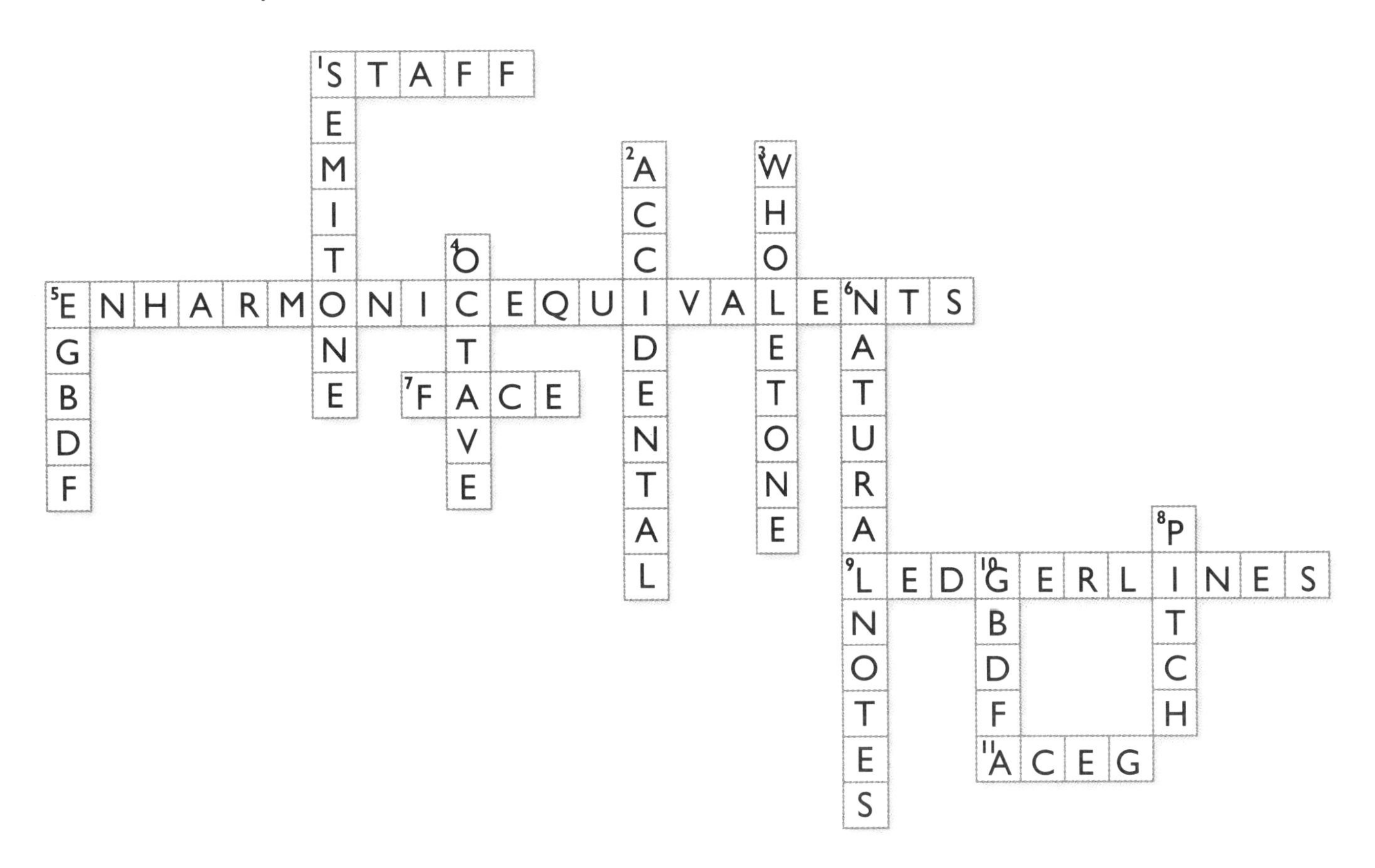

Daily Exercises for Chapter 1

EXERCISES FOR DAY 1

Re-read chapter 1 and complete the following exercises:

Exercise 1.1

Provide the letter names for each specified key marked on the keyboard.

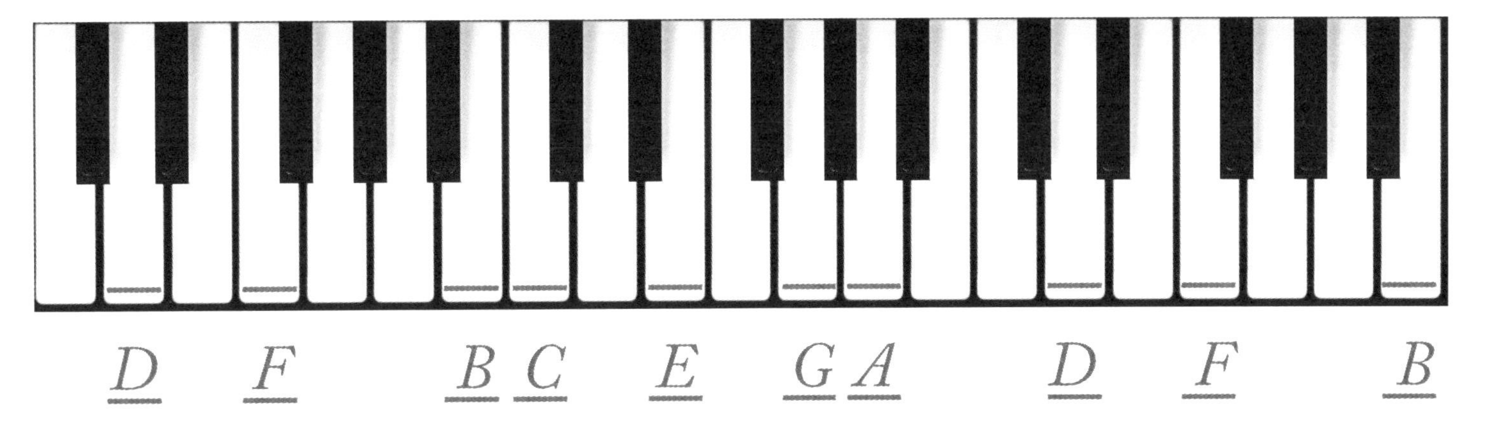

Exercise 1.2

Provide the name for each black note marked on the keyboard and include its enharmonic equivalent name.

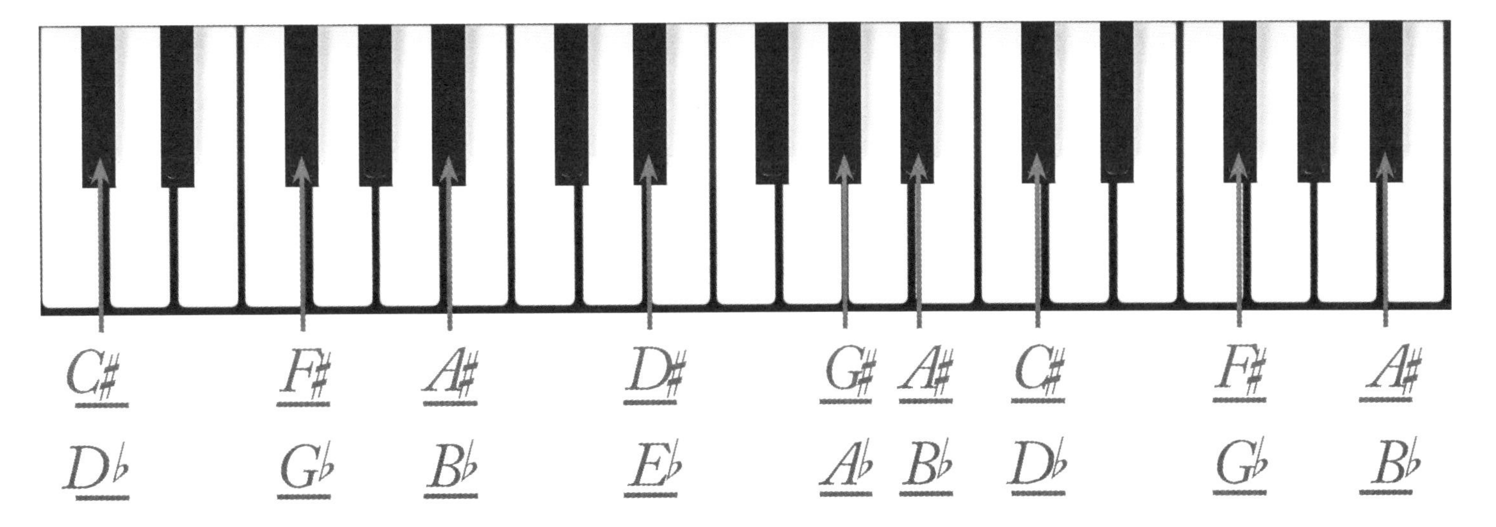

Exercise 1.3

Use arrows to show motions of whole or half steps.

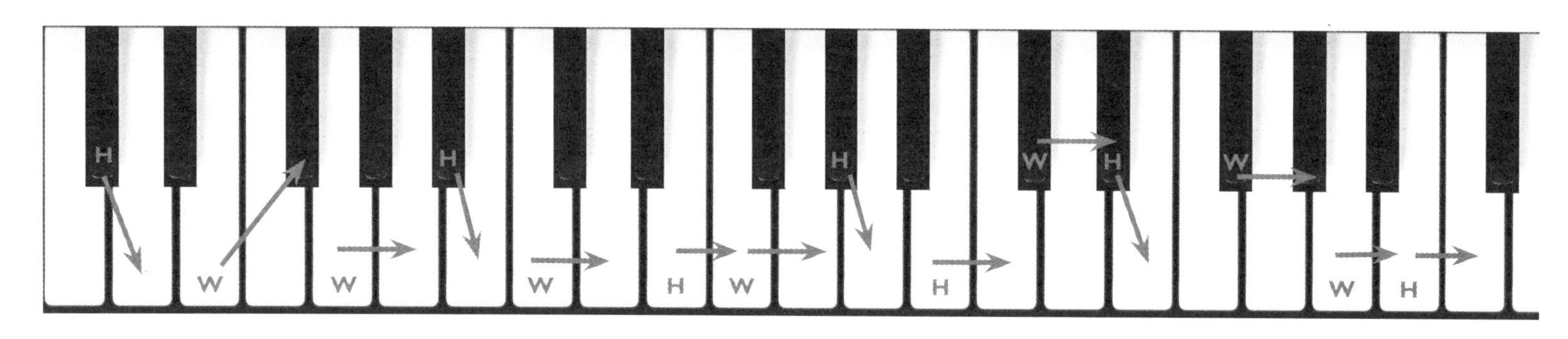

Exercise 1.4

On the staff below, write flat signs in front of notes in the first two measures, sharp signs in front of the notes in the second and third measures, and natural signs in front of the notes in the final two measures.

Exercise 1.5

Give the note enharmonically equivalent to each of the following notes:

a) B♯ C b) D♭ C♯ c) E♮ F♭ d) E♭ D♯

e) G♯ A♭ f) A♭ G♯ g) F♯ G♭ h) C♮ B♯

EXERCISES FOR DAY 2

Re-read chapter 1 and complete the following exercises:

Exercise 1.6

Practice drawing the symbols for a treble and bass clef on the following staves:

Exercise 1.7

Name the following notes on the treble clef:

Name the following notes on the bass clef:

Exercise 1.8

Draw arrows from the treble clef set of notes to the correct key on the keyboard.

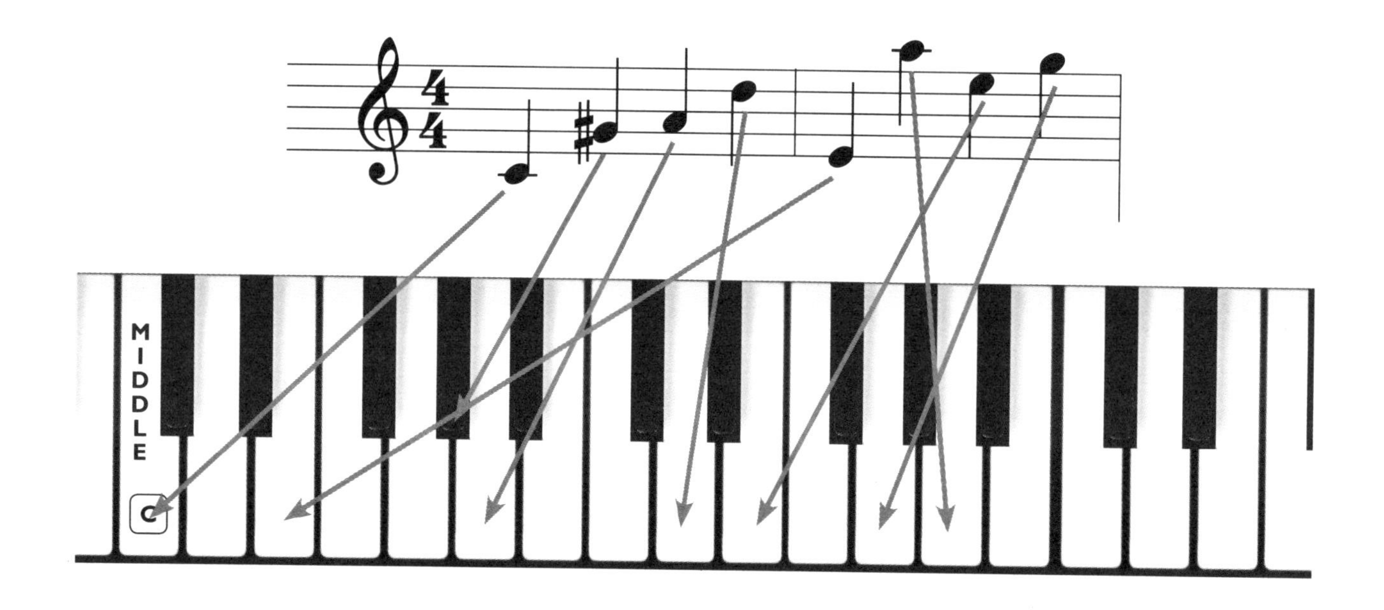

Draw arrows from the bass clef set of notes to the correct key on the keyboard.

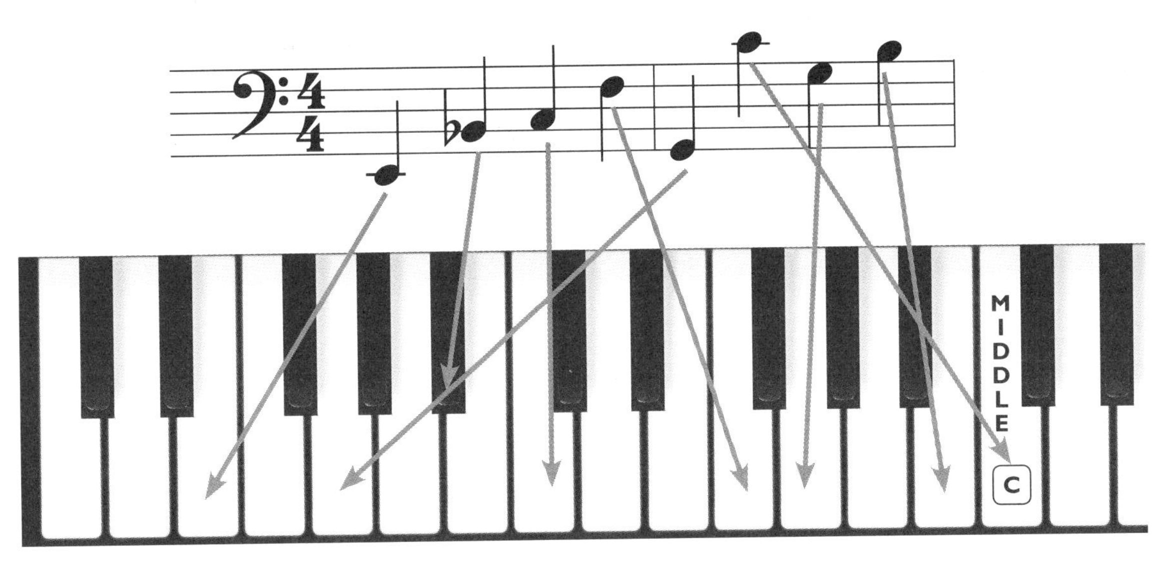

EXERCISES FOR DAY 3

The figures in the following exercises are excerpts from the scores at the end of your book. Refer to the scores to guide you through these exercises.

Exercise 1.9

The following excerpt is the third line on the treble clef of the hymn "When Peace Like a River." Label these notes with the correct note names.

Exercise 1.10

The following excerpt is the third line on the bass clef of the hymn "When Peace Like a River." Identify the numbered notes by writing their numbers on the keyboard below.

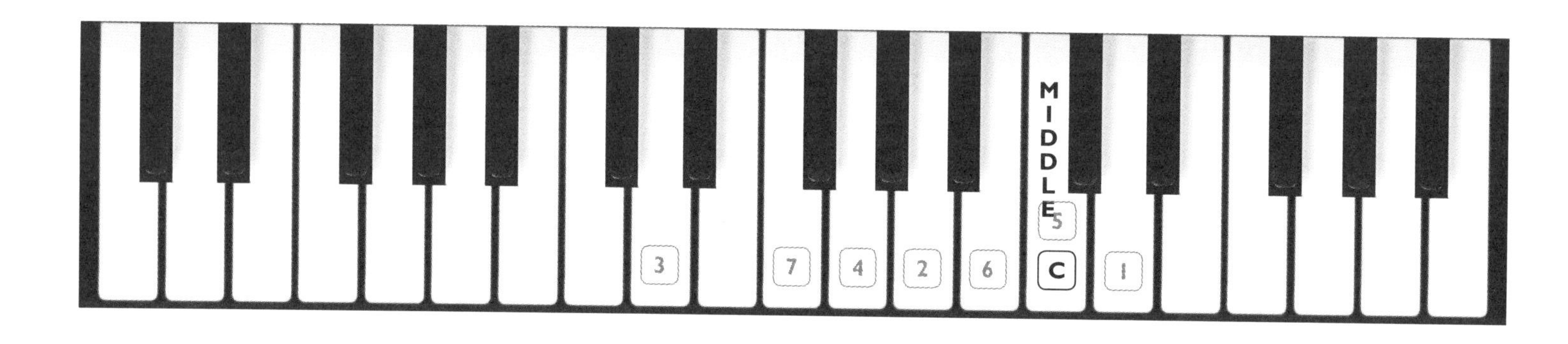

EXERCISES FOR DAY 4

Exercise 1.11

Write the following notes on the treble clef (there can be more than one correct answer).

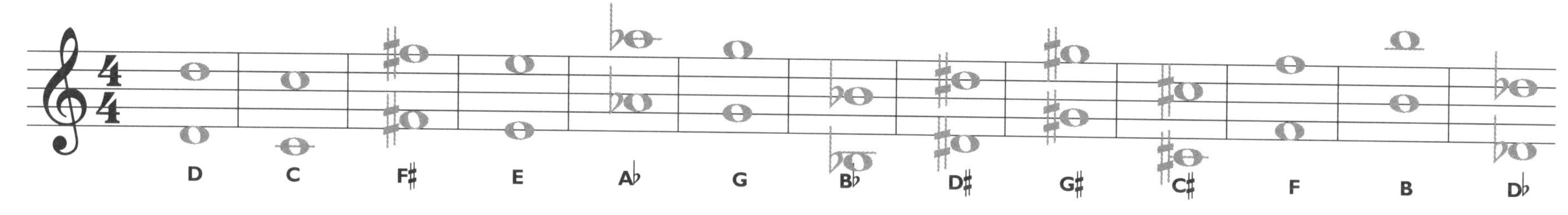

Exercise 1.12

Write the following notes on the bass clef:

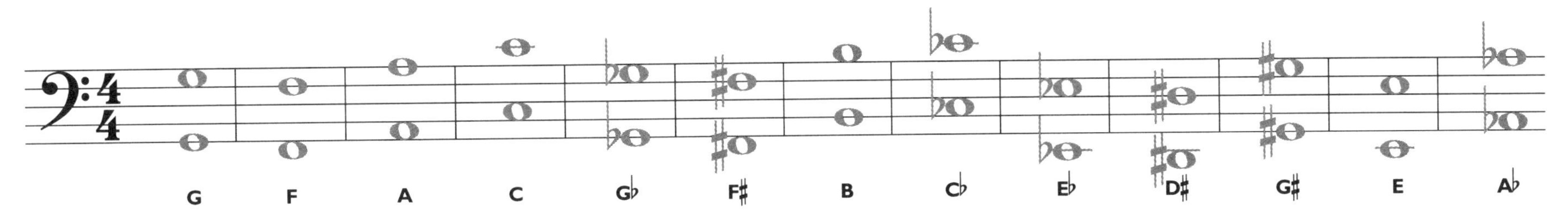

Exercise 1.13

Draw arrows from the notes on the staff to their corresponding keys on the keyboard (MC=middle C).

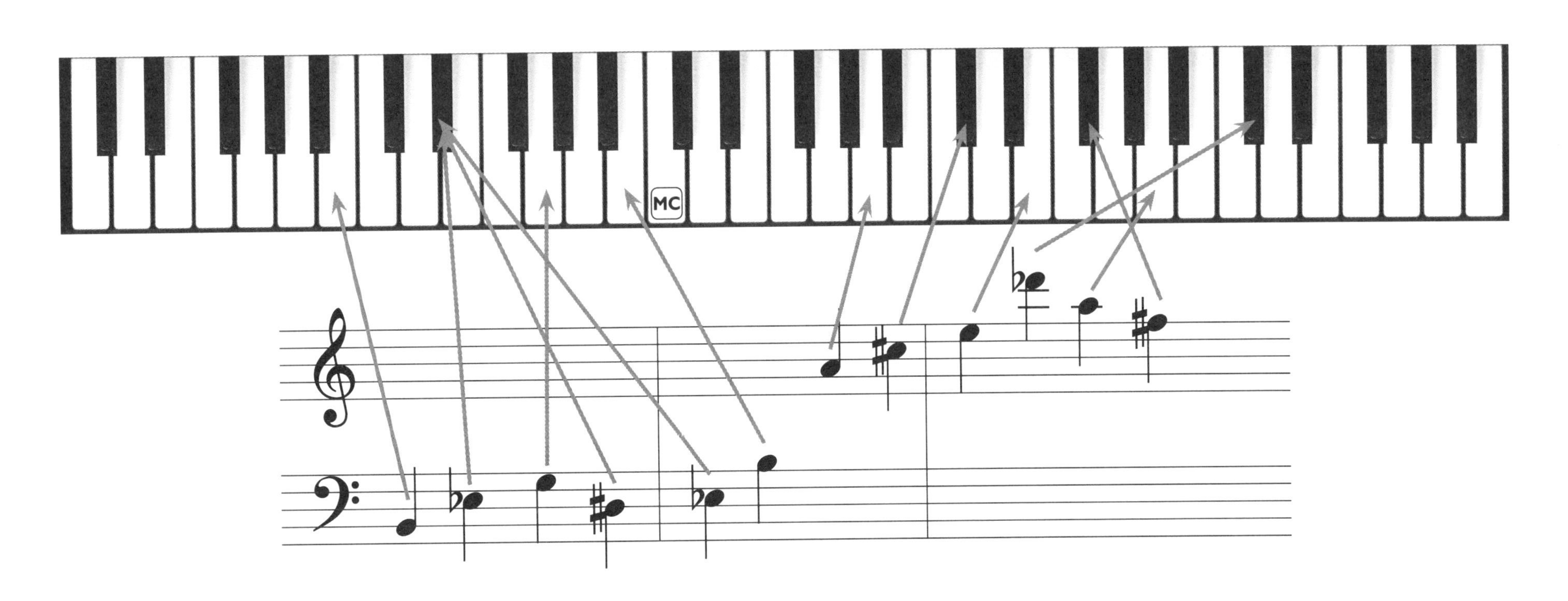

Exercise 1.14

Notate each note with an "x" on the staff provided below. Once notated, draw arrows from the notes on the keyboard to their corresponding notes on the staff (MC = middle C).

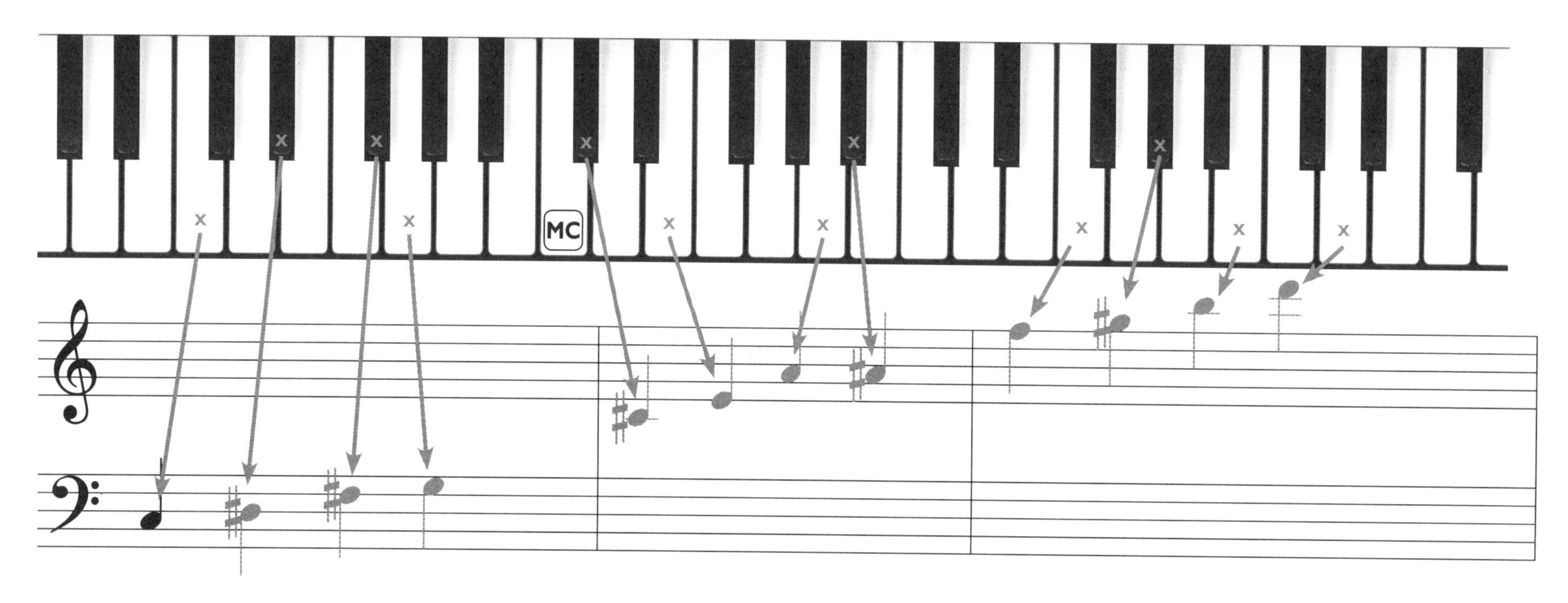

or

Exercise 1.15

Use the keyboard below to mark the following notes and specific octaves:

a) Label all of the C notes on the keyboard with a C right below each key.

b) Label all of the F# notes on the keyboard with an F# right above each key.

c) Label all the G octaves on the keyboard with a G and the correct octave number on each key.

d) Label all the E octaves on the keyboard with an E and the correct octave number on each key.

e) Mark the notes on the keyboard that do not belong to any octave charts by writing an "x" on the notes.

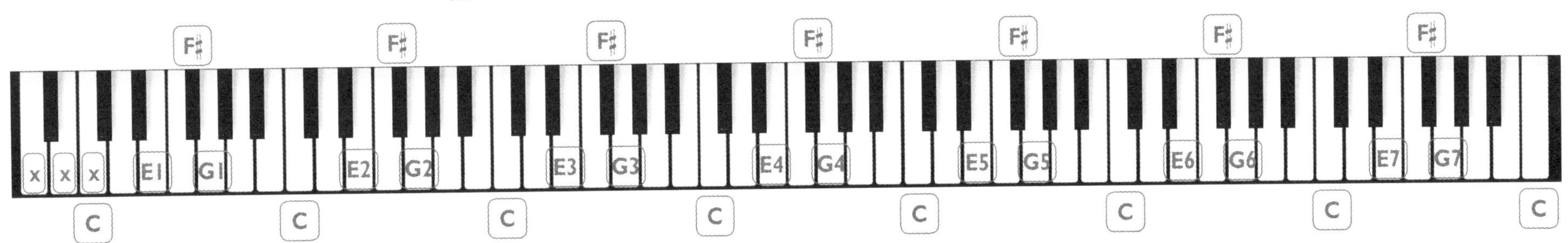

2 Music Grammar Part 2: Symbols and Notes

Chapter 2 Review

E R U T A N G I S E M I T
K E Y S I G N A T U R E V
X M W H O L E L Q D X T D
P E A T A M R E F T O L V
R A B E L B U O D T T W D
E S X A A R J R A I D D L
T U L M R C E C E T J X Z
R R L U F L C P J S Y L X
A E T L R A I E E L T K V
U W A Y T M W N N A X K Y
Q H N S D W P D E T T G V

Daily Exercises for Chapter 2

EXERCISES FOR DAY 1

Read through chapter 2 and complete the following exercises:

Exercise 2.1

Name the following symbols:

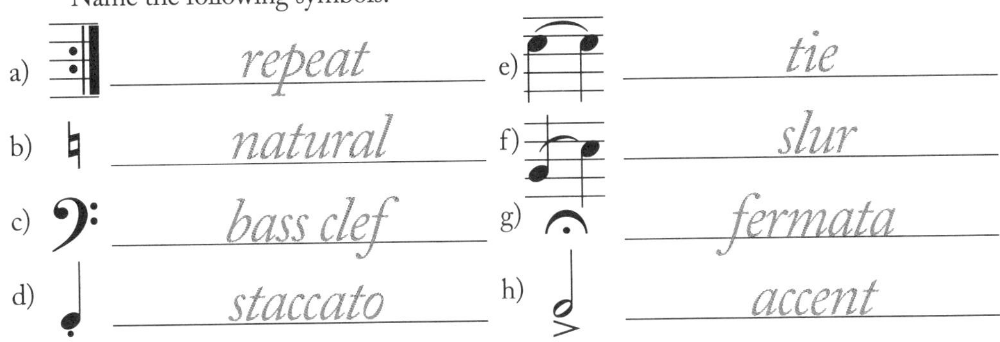

Exercise 2.2

Answer the following questions about the hymn score of "Old Hundredth" (Doxology) found in the Hymn Score Anthology, page 255.

a) How many **fermata** signs are found in the score (both bass and treble clefs)? 6

b) How many **measures** are in the score? (Do not count the first measure with the first set of quarter notes in it.) 8

c) What is the **time signature** of the score? 4/4

d) How many **sharp signs** are in the key signature? 1

e) How many times is **F♯** played in the score? 12

f) Not including the notes with fermata signs, how many **different note values** can you find in the score? 2

EXERCISES FOR DAY 2

Review chapter 2 and complete the following exercises:

Exercise 2.3

Answer the following questions, and prepare to do some math.

a) How many half notes make up one whole note? 2

b) How many quarter notes make up one half note? 2

c) How many eighth notes make up one half note? 4

d) How many sixteenth notes make up one whole note? 16

e) How many sixteenth notes make up four eighth notes? 8

f) How many eighth notes make up four half notes? 16

g) How many quarter notes make up four whole notes? 16

h) Thirty-two sixteenth notes make up how many whole notes? 2

i) Sixteen quarter notes make up how many half notes? 8

j) Thirty-two eighth notes make up how many half notes? 8

Exercise 2.4

Write a single note equal to the following sets of notes.

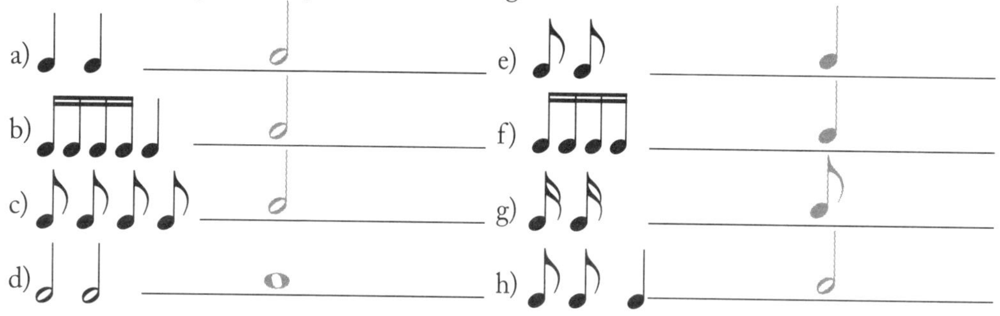

EXERCISES FOR DAY 3

Review chapter 2 and complete the following exercises:

Exercise 2.5

Write two notes whose combined value is equal to the following sets of notes: (Remember, these could have more than one correct answer. For example, a whole note is equal to two half notes or a dotted half note plus a quarter note, etc.)

a) (4) = ____ + ____
d) (½) = ____ + ____
b) (2) = ____ + ____
e) (1) = ____ + ____
c) (1) = ____ + ____
f) (2) = ____ + ____

Exercise 2.6

Draw the corresponding rest sign next to the following notes:

a) = ____
d) = ____
b) = ____
e) = ____
c) = ____

Exercise 2.7

Draw a single rest equal to the following sets of notes:

a) = ____
e) = ____
b) = ____
f) = ____
c) = ____
g) = ____
d) = ____
h) = ____

EXERCISES FOR DAY 4

Review chapter 2 and complete the following exercises:

Exercise 2.8

In the blank staff, rewrite the notes below using the following criteria:

a) Using only eighth notes, recreate the notes in the first measure without changing the total note value for the measure.

b) Using quarter notes, recreate the notes in the second measure without changing the total note value for the measure.

c) Make the third measure set of notes represent nothing but sixteenth notes.

d) Make the fourth measure set of notes represent nothing but half notes.

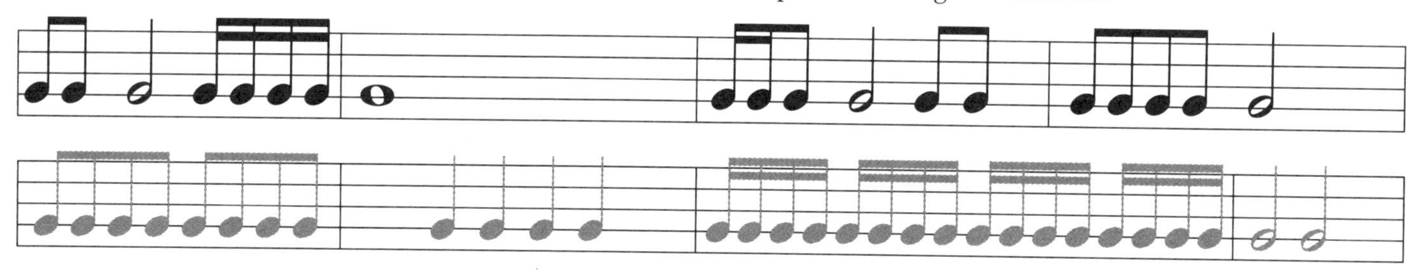

Exercise 2.9

Use the open staves below to complete the following steps:

a) Draw a treble clef at the beginning of the staff with a $\frac{4}{4}$ time signature.

b) Using bar lines, divide the staff into five measures, ending with a double bar line.

c) Use only quarter notes in the first two measures to write a melody. Be sure to name these notes below the staff and write only four quarter notes in each measure.

d) Use only half notes in the third and fourth measures to write a melody. Be sure to name these notes below the staff and write only two half notes in each measure.

e) In the last measure, include a half rest and a half note. Be sure to name the note below the staff.

f) Write in a repeat sign at the end of the last measure on the staff.

3 Introduction to Rhythm

Chapter 3 Review

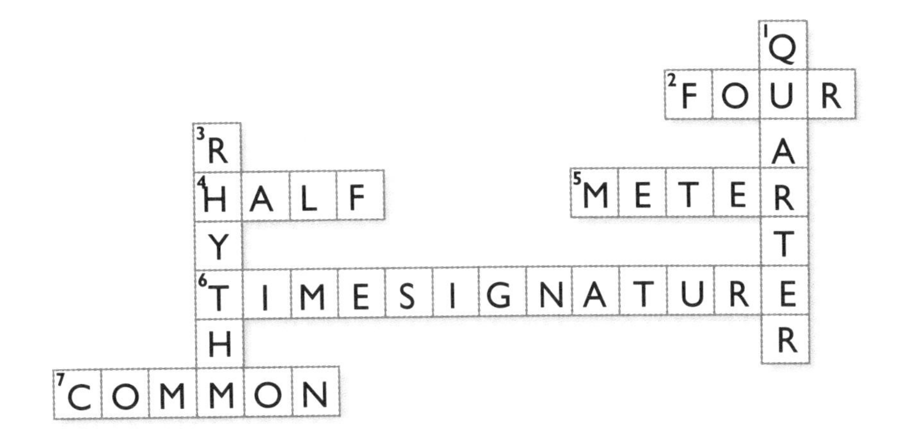

Daily Exercises for Chapter 3

EXERCISES FOR DAY 1

Exercise 3.1

Read through chapter 3 and answer the following questions:

a) What is the rhythm? What is meter? *Rhythm is the measure of musical movements in time. Meter is the grouping of musical rhythms.*

b) What type of note gets the beat in common meter? What symbol is used to show common meter? *The quarter note gets the beat in common meter. The symbol to show common meter is* **C**.

c) How many beats are in each measure of common meter? *4*

d) In a given score, what is used to indicate which type of note serves as the beat and how many beats are in each measure? *time signature*

e) In a given time signature, what does the top number communicate? What does the bottom number communicate? *In time signature, the top number gives the number of beats per measure. The bottom number represents what type of note (value) serves as the beat.*

Exercise 3.2

Answer the following questions about the different time signatures:

(a) 3/2 (b) 3/4 (c) 2/4 (d) 3/8 (e) **C**

1) What time signature has the eighth note getting the beat? *d*

2) What time signature has the half note getting the beat? *a*

3) How many quarter notes are in each measure of time signature (b)? *3*

4) How many quarter notes are in each measure of time signature (e)? *4*

5) Explain what the top and bottom number communicate in time signature (d):

top: *The top number in (d) denotes 3 beats per measure.*

bottom: *The bottom number in (d) denotes that the eighth note gets the beat.*

6) Explain what the top and bottom number communicate in time signature (c):

top: *The top number in (c) denotes 2 beats per measure.*

bottom: *The bottom number in (c) denotes that the quarter note gets the beat.*

7) What time signature is $\frac{4}{4}$ timing? *common meter*

EXERCISES FOR DAY 2

Exercise 3.3

Practice reading rhythms by clapping or counting aloud the following note values in common meter. Use the numbers below to count the rhythms correctly.

Full beat counting practice

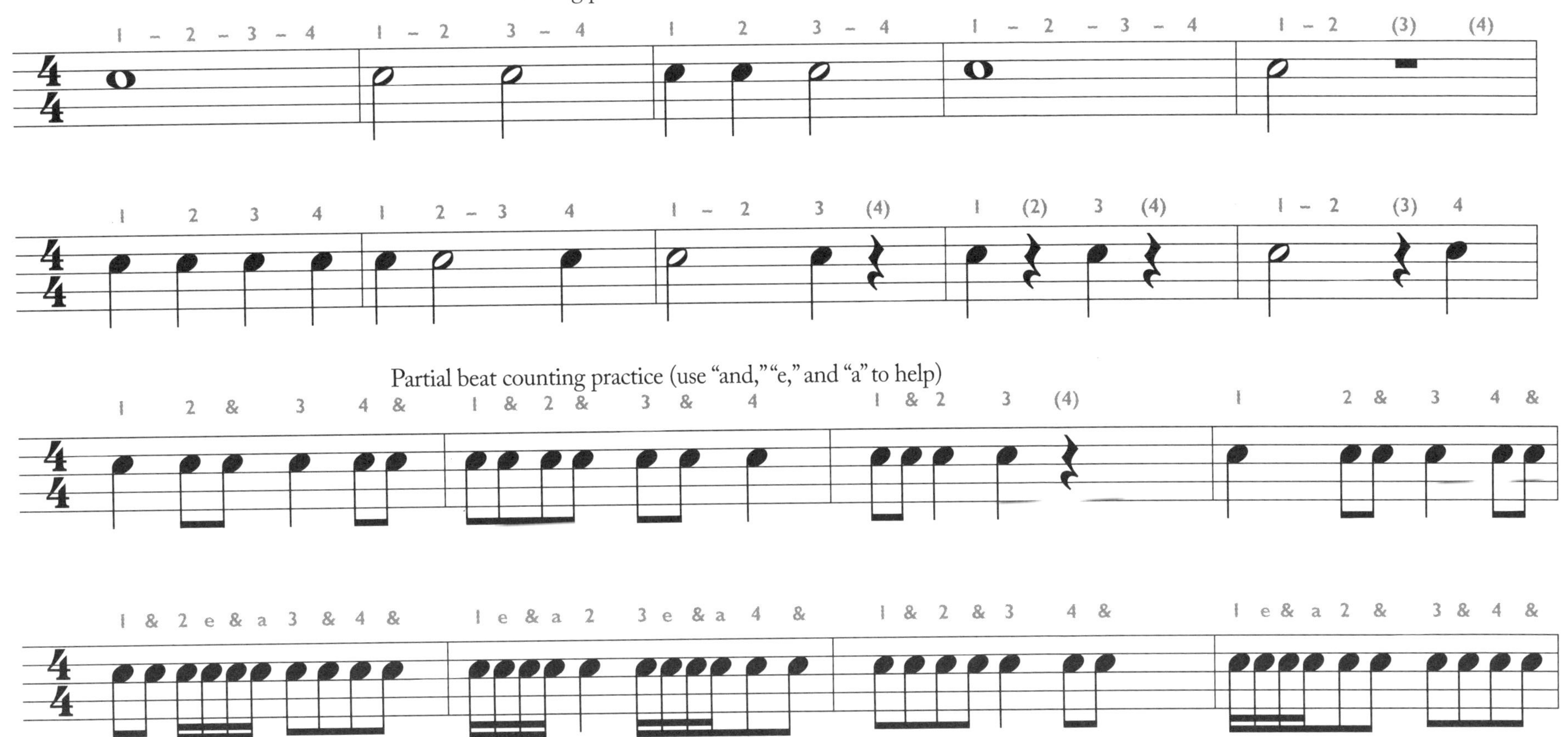

Exercise 3.4

The following excerpt is the first and second line from the hymn "When I Survey the Wondrous Cross." Complete the following using the excerpt.

a) Write the correct number of beats above each individual note or pair of notes on the treble clef.

b) Practice reading rhythm by counting or clapping the treble clef melody aloud.

EXERCISES FOR DAY 3

Exercise 3.5

Fill in the correct note values to complete the following measures so that they match the time signature.

Exercise 3.6

Practice reading rhythms by counting or clapping the following note values in common meter. Numbers below are for helpful counting

Exercise 3.7

Answer the following questions about dotted notes:

a) How many quarter notes would be of equal value to one dotted whole note? 6

b) How many dotted eighth notes would be of equal value to six quarter notes? 8

c) How many sixteenth notes would be of equal value to three dotted eighth notes? 9

d) How many dotted half notes would be of equal value to two dotted whole notes? 4

EXERCISES FOR DAY 4

Exercise 3.8

Practice reading rhythms by clapping these dotted notes in common meter.

Exercise 3.9

Answer the following questions about the excerpt from the hymn "It Is Well with My Soul." Please note that the second musical line of this exercise is meant to be optional for students.

a) Starting with the first full measure, write the correct number of beats above each individual note or pair of notes on the treble clef.

b) Practice reading rhythm by counting or clapping the treble clef melody aloud.

c) Label the name of every note on this excerpt to the right of each note.

d) Label all the different musical symbols we have learned.

4 Time Signature and Simple Meter

Chapter 4 Review

e 1. Simple meter

d 2. Duple meter

f 3. Time signature

a 4. Triple meter

g 5. Quadruple meter

c 6. Top number in time signature

b 7. Bottom number in time signature

a. Meter in which each measure is divided into three beats

b. Indicates which type of note serves as the beat

c. Indicates how many beats there are per measure

d. Meter in which the measure is divided into two beats

e. Meter in which each beat in a measure can be subdivided by two

f. The numbers or signs placed on the staff to indicate the meter of the measures

g. Meter in which each measure is divided into four beats

Daily Exercises for Chapter 4

EXERCISES FOR DAY 1

Exercise 4.1

Read through chapter 4 and answer the following questions:

a) In simple meter, every beat can be subdivided by what number?

2

b) In simple time signatures, what does the top number mean?

the number of beats in each measure

c) In simple time signatures, what does the bottom number mean?

the type of note (value) that gets the beat

d) How many beats are in simple duple meter?

2

e) How many beats are in simple triple meter?

3

f) How many beats are in simple quadruple meter?

4

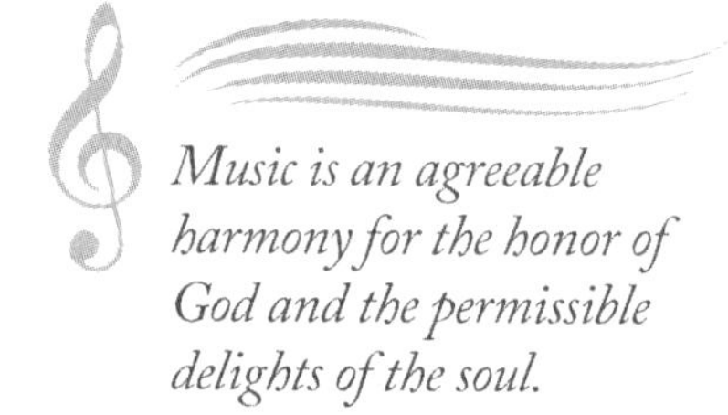

Music is an agreeable harmony for the honor of God and the permissible delights of the soul.

—Johann Sebastian Bach

Exercise 4.2

Match the following time signatures with the correct simple meter.

a) Duple   b) Triple   c) Quadruple

(1) *a* $\frac{2}{4}$ (2) *b* $\frac{3}{8}$ (3) *c* $\frac{4}{8}$ (4) *b* $\frac{3}{4}$

(5) *b* $\frac{3}{2}$ (6) *c* $\frac{4}{2}$ (7) *c* $\frac{4}{4}$ (8) *a* $\frac{2}{2}$

(9) *a* $\frac{2}{8}$ (10) *b* $\frac{3}{4}$ (11) *a* $\frac{2}{2}$ (12) *b* $\frac{3}{2}$

EXERCISES FOR DAY 2

Exercise 4.3

Use the excerpt below of the first line of the hymn "Be Thou My Vision" to answer the following questions:

a) In the figure above, which note value gets the beat? *quarter note*

b) Is the meter above simple duple, triple, or quadruple? *triple*

c) Practice counting rhythm by clapping the melody of the piece above.

Exercise 4.4

Insert bar lines to complete the measures in the requested meter.

a) Insert bar lines below to complete the measures for $\frac{2}{4}$ meter.

b) Insert bar lines below to complete the measures for $\frac{3}{2}$ meter.

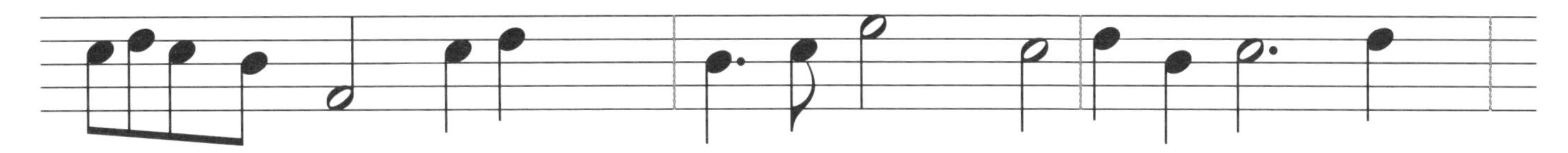

EXERCISES FOR DAY 3

Exercise 4.5

Use the excerpt below of the first line of the hymn "There Is A Fountain Filled with Blood" to answer the following questions:

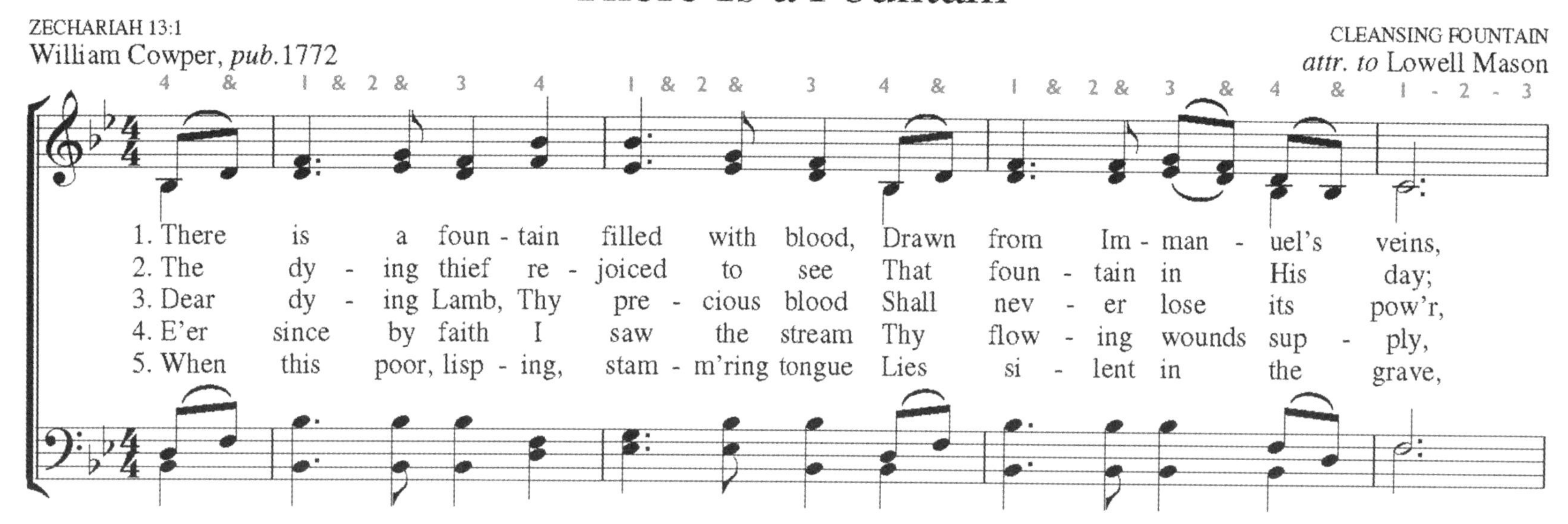

a) How many beats are in the last measure of the line above? How many beats are in the very beginning partial measure of the line above? (This is called an **anacrusis.**)

last line: 3 beats first line (anacrusis): 1 beat

b) Is the meter above duple, triple, or quadruple meter?

quadruple

c) Practice counting rhythm by clapping the main melody of this first line while singing/counting the correct meter. See numbers above for counting.

Exercise 4.6

Fill in each incorrect measure with one or more notes of the correct note value that corresponds with the given meter.

EXERCISES FOR DAY 4

Exercise 4.7

Complete the following measures in each meter by composing different rhythm combinations. Be ready to clap, tap, AND count your rhythm compositions at the beginning of next class.

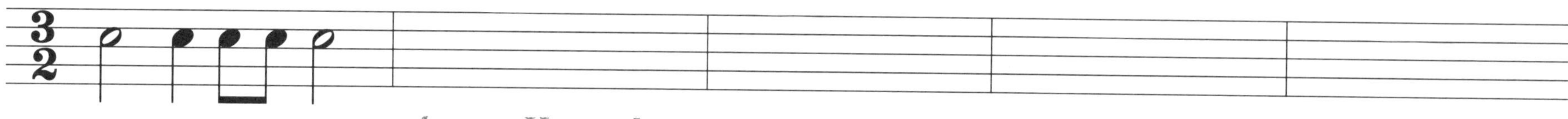

Answer Key: each measure must add up to three half notes or six quarter notes.

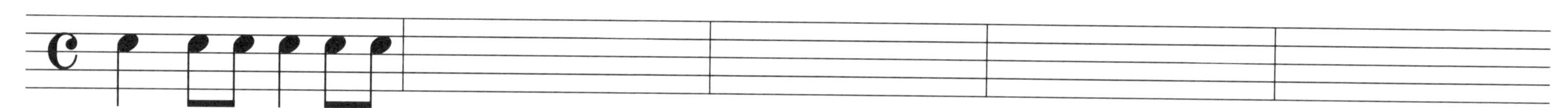

Answer Key: each measure must add up to two half notes or four quarter notes.

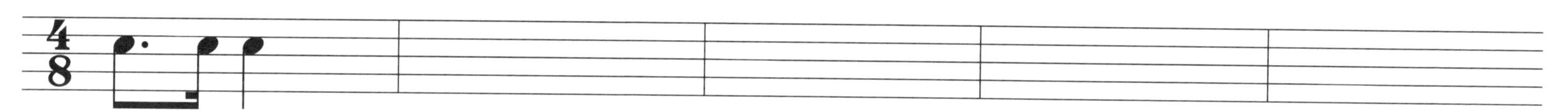

Answer Key: each measure must add up to two quarter notes or four eighth notes.

5 Major and Natural Minor Scales

Chapters 1–5 Review

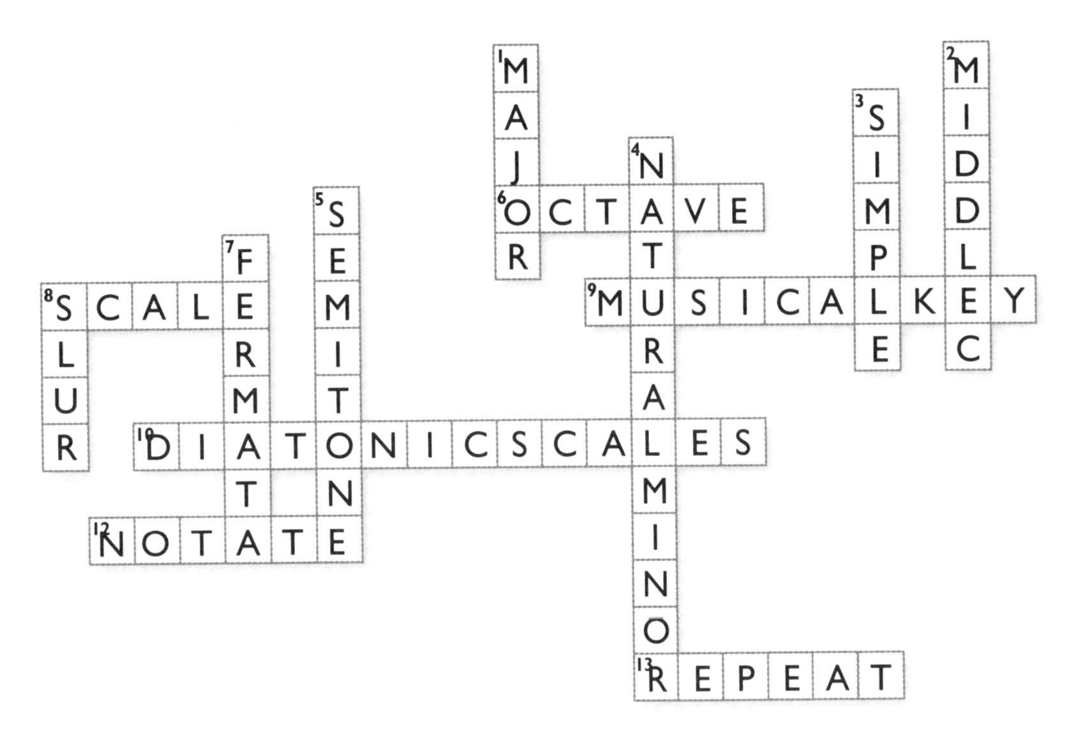

Daily Exercises for Chapter 5

EXERCISES FOR DAY 1

Exercise 5.1

Read through chapter 5 and answer the following questions:

a) What scale system do we use in Western music?

diatonic

b) If both the major and minor scales contain eight notes, what is the difference between major and minor scales?

the whole and half step patterns

c) What is the pattern of whole tones and semitones for major scales?

W–W–H–W–W–W–H

d) What is the pattern of whole tones and semitones for natural minor scales?

W–H–W–W–H–W–W

e) What is the term for the distance between two notes with the same name?

octave

Exercise 5.2

Practice recognizing whole tones and semitones on a staff by labeling the following distances between the pairs of notes in each measure as either a whole step (whole tone) or a half step (semitone).

1.

H *W* *H* *H* *H*

There are a number of different answers to exercise 5.2.2. For whole steps, remember that the two notes must be separated by two semitones. For half steps, the two notes must be separated by one semitone.

2. Write your own pairs of notes with the indicated half step or whole step. There is no key, so indicate sharps and flats, if needed.

whole step **half step** **whole step** **whole step** **half step**

Exercise 5.3

Fill in the missing notes to the scales given below by notating them on the staff.

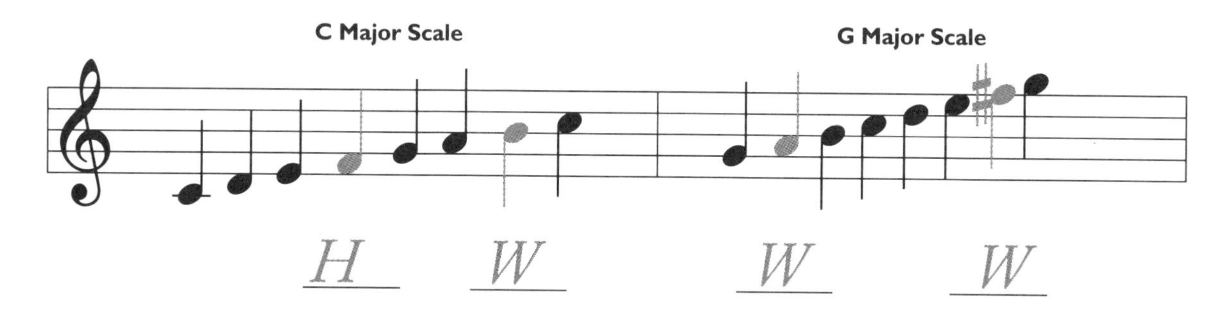

Label each note you just notated as either a whole or half step from the note before it.

EXERCISES FOR DAY 2

Exercise 5.4

Fill in the missing notes in the following major scales. Use the keyboard sheet in the back of your book if you need to.

1. D E F♯ G A B C♯ D
2. A B C♯ D E F♯ G♯ A
3. G A B C D E F♯ G
4. B♭ C D E♭ F G A B♭
5. F G A B♭ C D E F
6. E F♯ G♯ A B C♯ D♯ E

Take two scales from above and notate the scales on the staves on the next page. Notate the scales in ascending and descending order, with one scale in the treble clef and one in the bass clef. If there are accidentals, place them to the left of the note.

D major
A major

G major
B♭ major

F major
E major

Exercise 5.5

Use the major and minor scale patterns of whole tones and semitones to answer the questions below (you might need to have your keyboard sheet).

a) How many sharps are in the D major scale? 2

b) How many flats are in the E♭ major scale? 3

c) How many flats are in the C natural minor scale? 3

d) How many sharps are in the F♯ natural minor scale? 3

EXERCISES FOR DAY 3

Exercise 5.6

In each example, the first note of the scale is given; notate the indicated major scale. Use sharps and flats to the left of the note if need be (no key signatures). Note: Once an accidental appears, it is assumed the accidental applies through the end of the measure unless notated otherwise.

Exercise 5.7

In each example, the first note of the scale is given; notate the indicated minor scale. Use sharps and flats to the left of the note if need be (no key signatures).

EXERCISES FOR DAY 4

Exercise 5.8

a) Write a melody in the following blank measures using only the notes that are sharped in the key of E major. You do not have to use sharp signs, as the key is assumed. Be sure to note the time signature.

Make sure that each measure contains note values that add up to three quarter notes.

3
4

b) Write a melody in the following blank measures using only the notes that are flatted in the key of A♭ major. You do not have to use flat signs, as the key is assumed. Be sure to note the time signature.

Make sure that each measure contains note values that add up to two half notes.

2
2

Exercise 5.9

Identify the following major or minor natural scales. Remember, descending scales use the pattern backwards. It might be helpful to label whole tones and semitones on the scale so you can identify major or minor correctly.

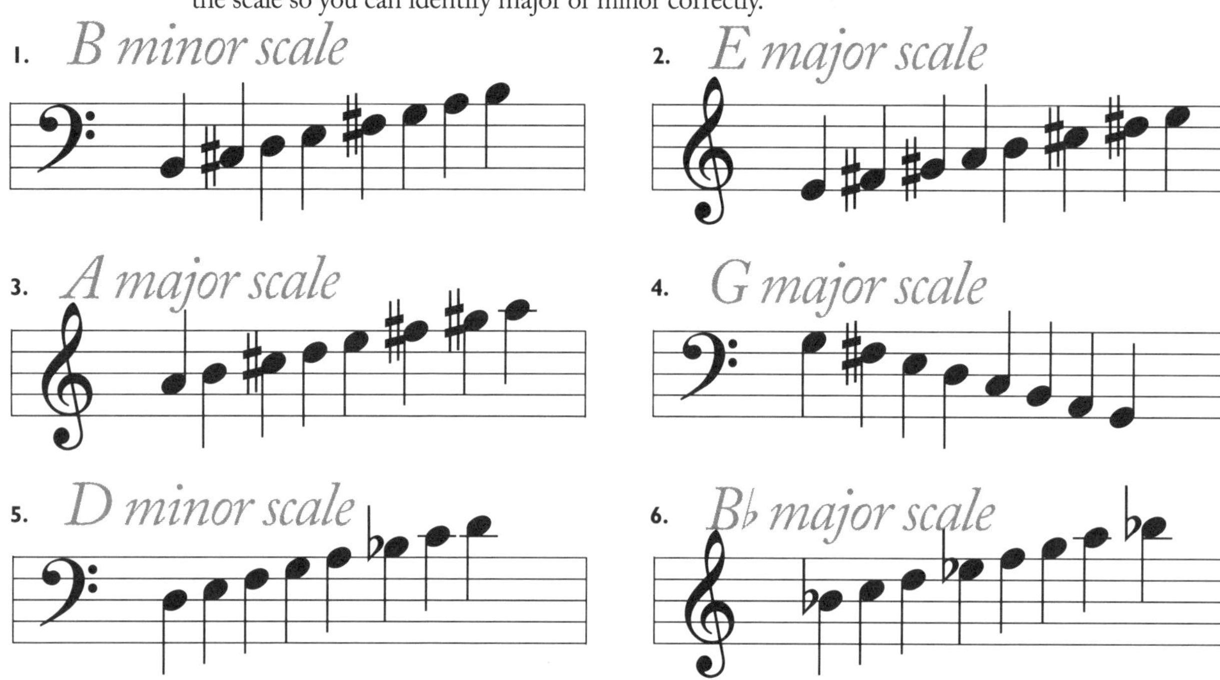

6 Key Signatures

Chapter 6 Review

E N H A R M O N I C E Q U I V A L E N T S
R N J J O F M A J O R R T Z Z Z X R Z B P
U D R T J T N P L K L L P R N L B W T K B
T L L N A K N L D M N L J Q Y D T G W X T
A D D N M R Y M V Q P J B Y G P L T B P R
N Q Z J B R G B L B Q J T Z Y W W R L D M
G N Y Y L L R N R D B R D L K T M P Y R Y
I N Y Z L Z Z J Q T E B B Z X M R D L W Y
S Q X X V J Y J Y L N T R V B Q O N T R Q
Y W N J X M T Y A J Z W D V N T J M K J P
E T K Q B Z X T T N X M Y V M J A M J Q Y
K J W B P M I R L R R F R Z D J M J D D M
G L J B E V M Z Q X W Z C Z R M A N M J W
G P K M E A D M Z R X G W G K M Q D G P R
G G P K B R D Y B Z D M V N D B N Z W N X
T R E V D Q Z G D L R X K W M A R L Q D B
N Y Y Z T V J J C Q R B Y Z L K E T D P X
S R J Y B W D G D F N V X Z V Q J B V B T

Daily Exercises for Chapter 6

EXERCISES FOR DAY 1

Exercise 6.1

Read through chapter 6 and answer the following questions:

a) How many key signatures are in our Western style of music?
12

b) What is a musical key? Give an example of a musical key.
The "space" where the music occurs; C major

c) Before reading a piece of music, what is the most important symbol you should know in order to read the notes of the score?
key signature

d) In the Circle of Fifths diagram, starting on C major, which direction do the key signatures with sharps move? Which direction do the key signatures with flats move?
clockwise; counterclockwise

e) What are enharmonic keys? Give an example, including the notes in the key.
Different key signatures with the same absolute pitches in their scales. Examples: B♭ major and A♯ major

Exercise 6.2

On the staves below and on the next page, write the indicated major key signature. Be sure to provide the correct order of sharps or flats within the key signature.

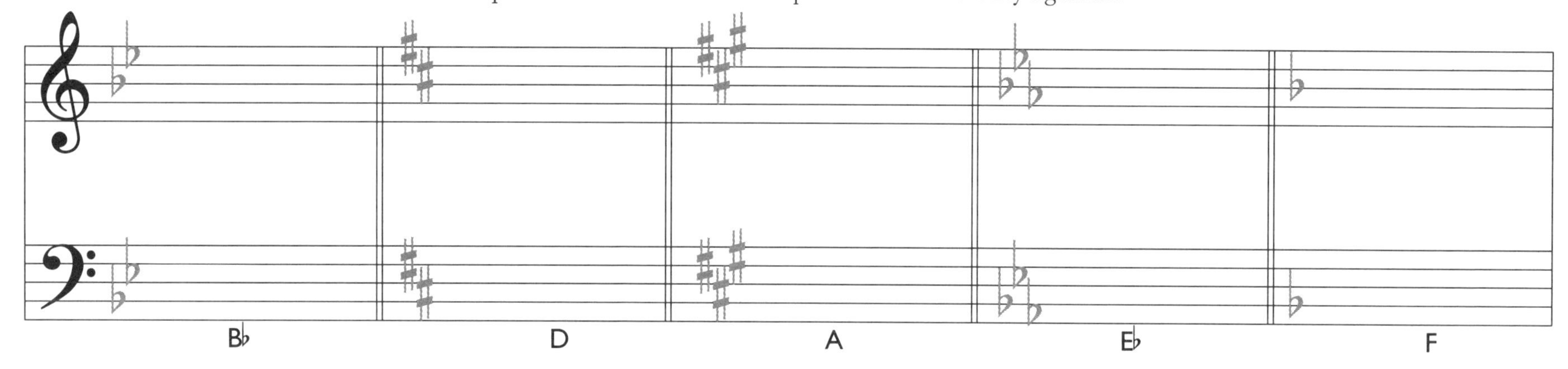

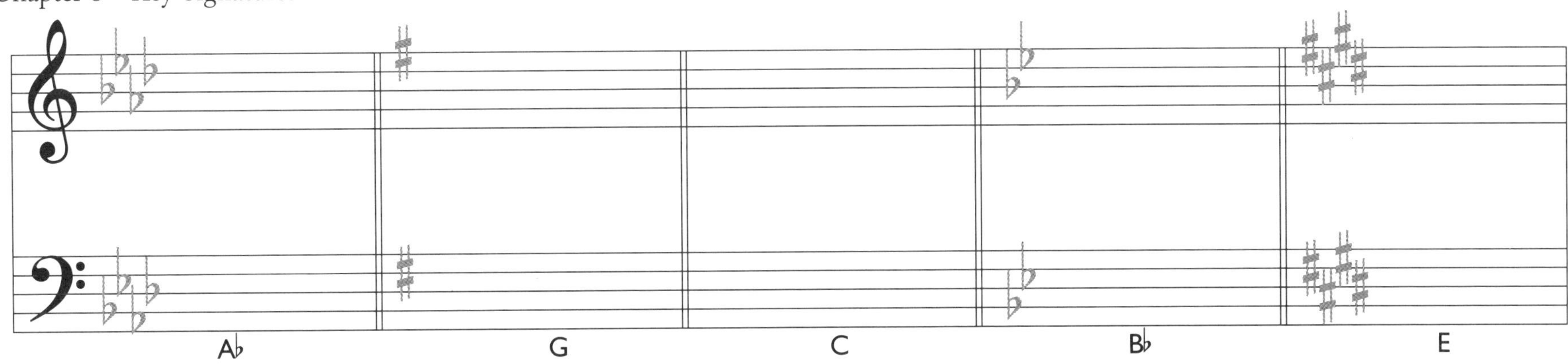

EXERCISES FOR DAY 2

Exercise 6.3

Use the key signature calculation method to answer the following questions:

a) If the key of D♭ major has five flats, D major must have how many sharps? 2

b) If the key of F major has one flat, F♯ major must have how many sharps? 6

c) If the key of A major has three sharps, A♭ major must have how many flats? 4

d) If the key of E major has four sharps, E♭ major must have how many flats? 3

e) If the key of B major has five sharps, B♭ major must have how many flats? 2

Exercise 6.4

Use the first line excerpt below from the hymn "Be Thou My Vision" to answer the questions below.

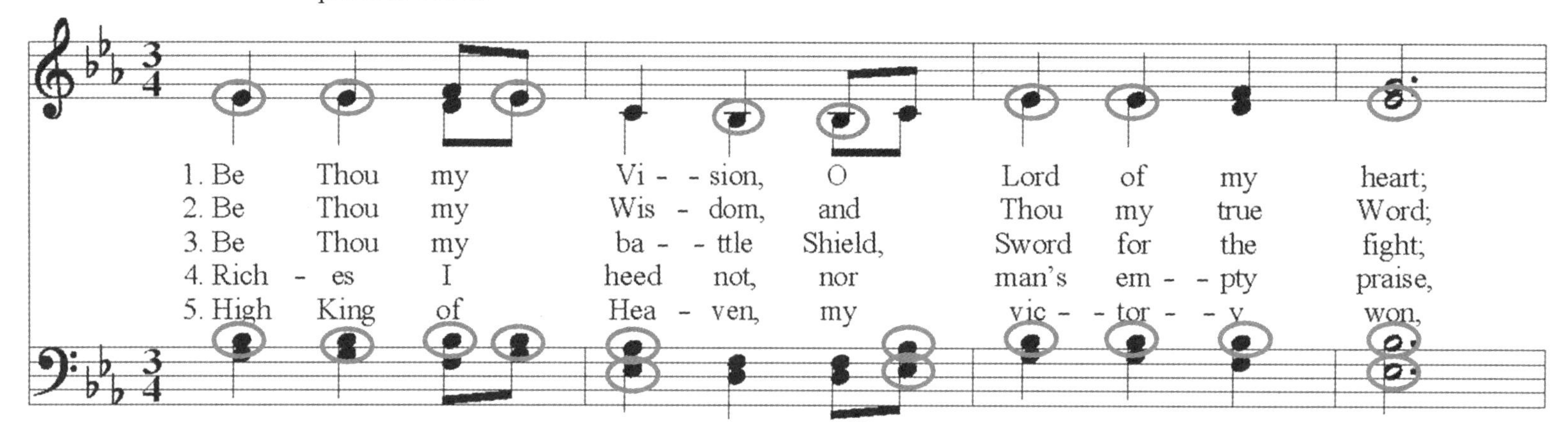

a) What key is the piece above in? *E♭ major*

b) Which notes are flatted in the key signature above? *B, E, A*

c) Which note value gets the beat? How many beats are in each measure?
quarter note; 3 beats in each measure

d) Circle all the notes in the piece in both the treble and bass clefs that are flats (key signature will help).

e) In the second measure, treble clef, is there a whole step or semitone step between the first two notes? *W*

EXERCISES FOR DAY 3

Exercise 6.5

Use the first line excerpt below from the hymn "When I Survey the Wondrous Cross" to answer the questions below.

a) What key is the excerpt above in? *F major*

b) What are the notes of the scale in the key above?
F–G–A–B♭–C–D–E–F

c) Circle all the notes in the piece in both the treble and bass clefs that are flats (key signature will help).

d) Which note in this first line is not in the key signature of the piece? How do you know it is not in the key?
F♯; the key is F major, which does not contain an F♯. We also know because the accidental (natural sign) is present.

e) Using the Circle of Fifths chart, which key going counterclockwise is after the key in this piece? How many flats or sharps are in this next key?
B♭ major; two flats

Exercise 6.6

Using the keyboard sheet in the back of your book and the three-semitone trick, match the relative keys.

1. ___c___ D minor
2. ___f___ C major
3. ___b___ E minor
4. ___e___ A major
5. ___a___ G minor
6. ___d___ D major

a) B♭ major
b) G major
c) F major
d) B minor
e) F♯ minor
f) A minor

EXERCISES FOR DAY 4

Exercise 6.7

On the staves below and on the next page, write the indicated minor key signature. Be sure to provide the correct order of sharps or flats within the key signature. It may be helpful to find the relative major key first in order to write the correct key signature for each minor key.

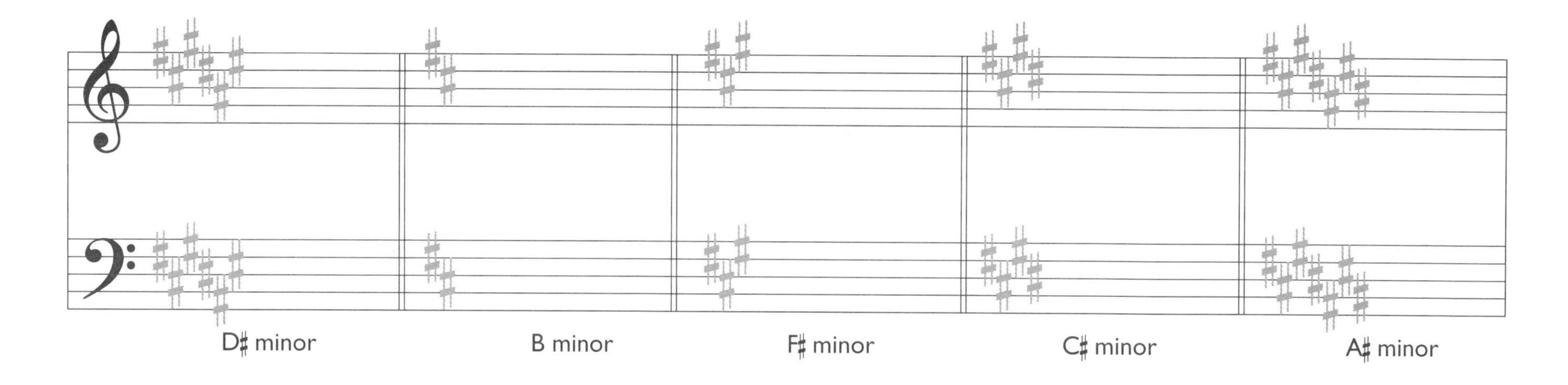

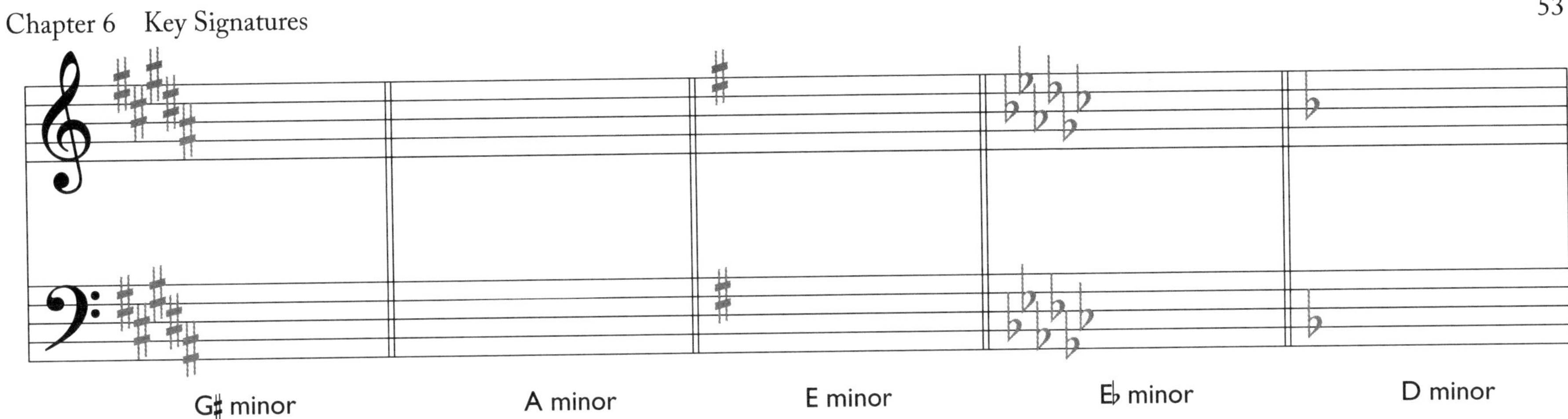

Exercise 6.8

Match the following key signatures to the correct key.

a) A minor b) C♯ major c) C minor d) E major e) D♭ major f) C♭ major
g) D♯ minor h) G♭ major i) B minor j) B major

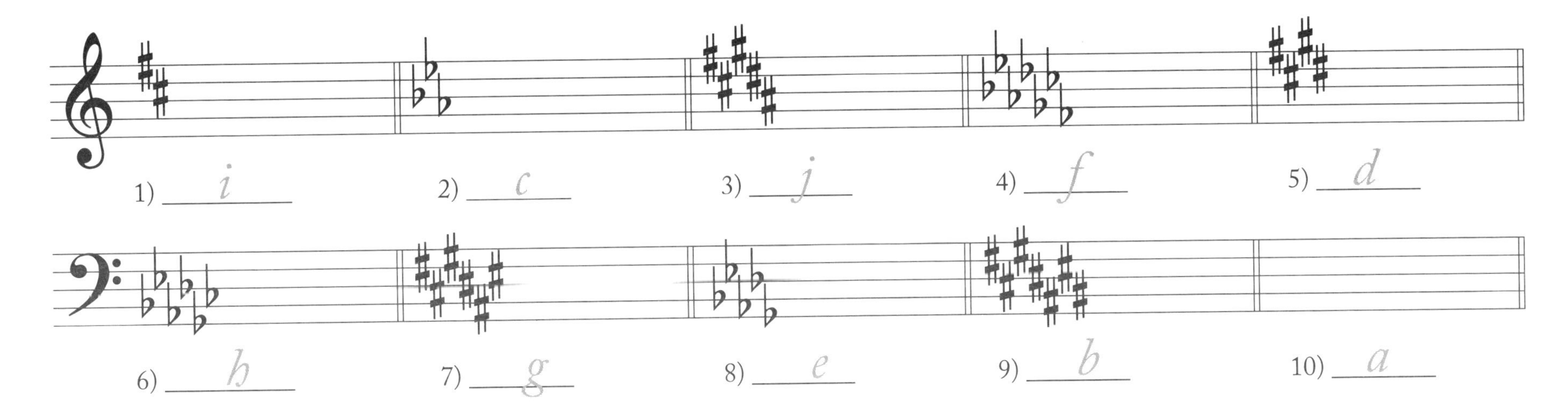

7 Scale Degrees and Transposing

Chapter 7 Review

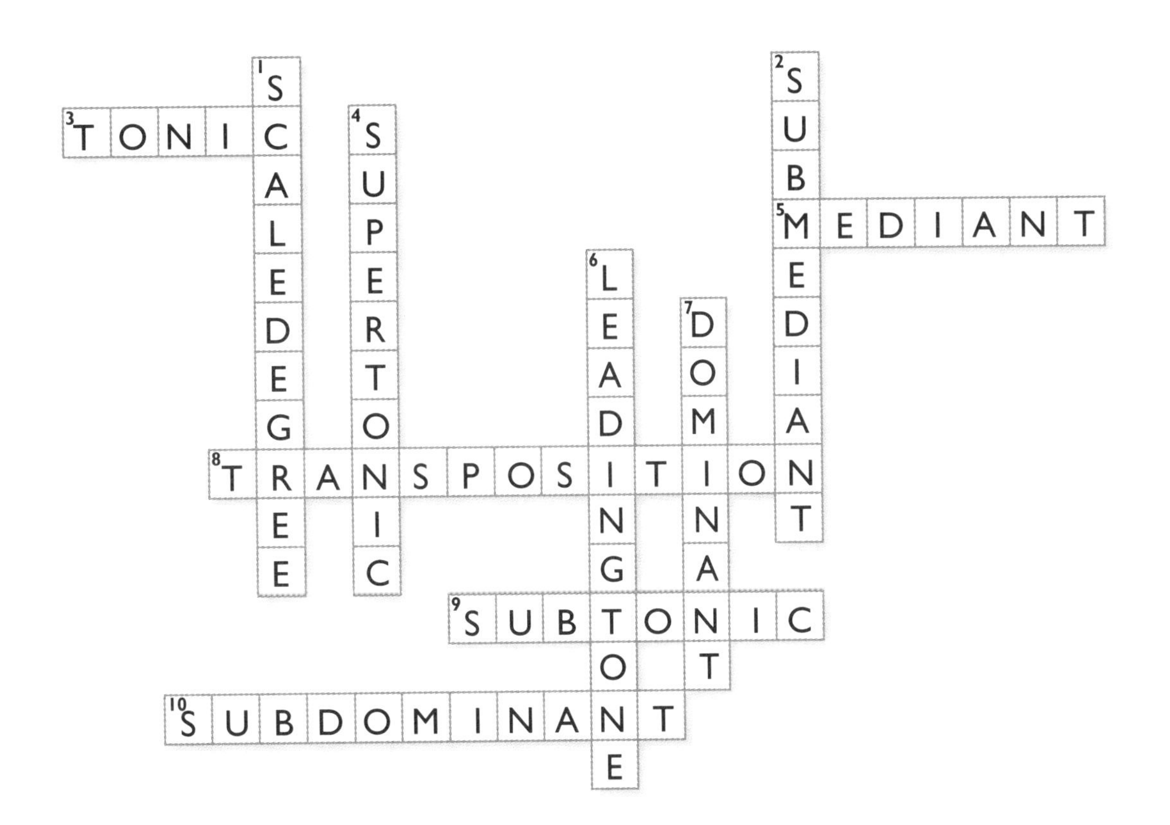

Daily Exercises for Chapter 7

EXERCISES FOR DAY 1

Exercise 7.1

Identify the major key and scale degree numbers for the following excerpts.

1) Bass of "Jesu, Joy of Man's Desiring"

Key: *G major*

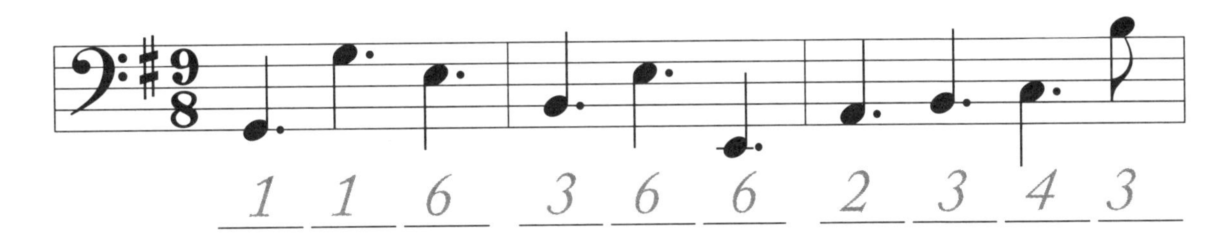

2) First line of "When I Survey the Wondrous Cross"

Key: *F major*

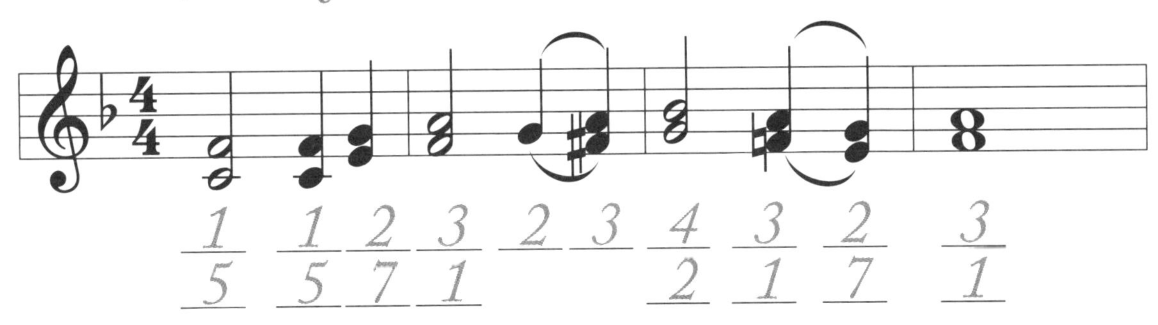

3) First line of "Be Thou My Vision"

Key: 

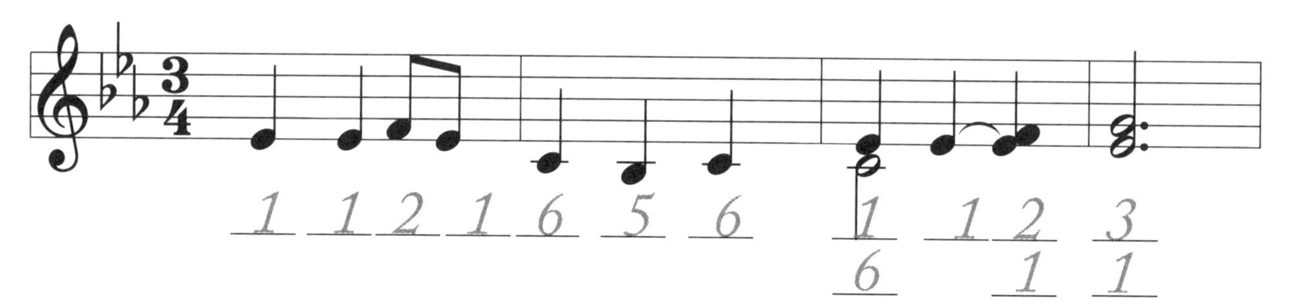

EXERCISES FOR DAY 2

Exercise 7.2

Identify the key and then write the correct note on the staff from the given scale degree name.

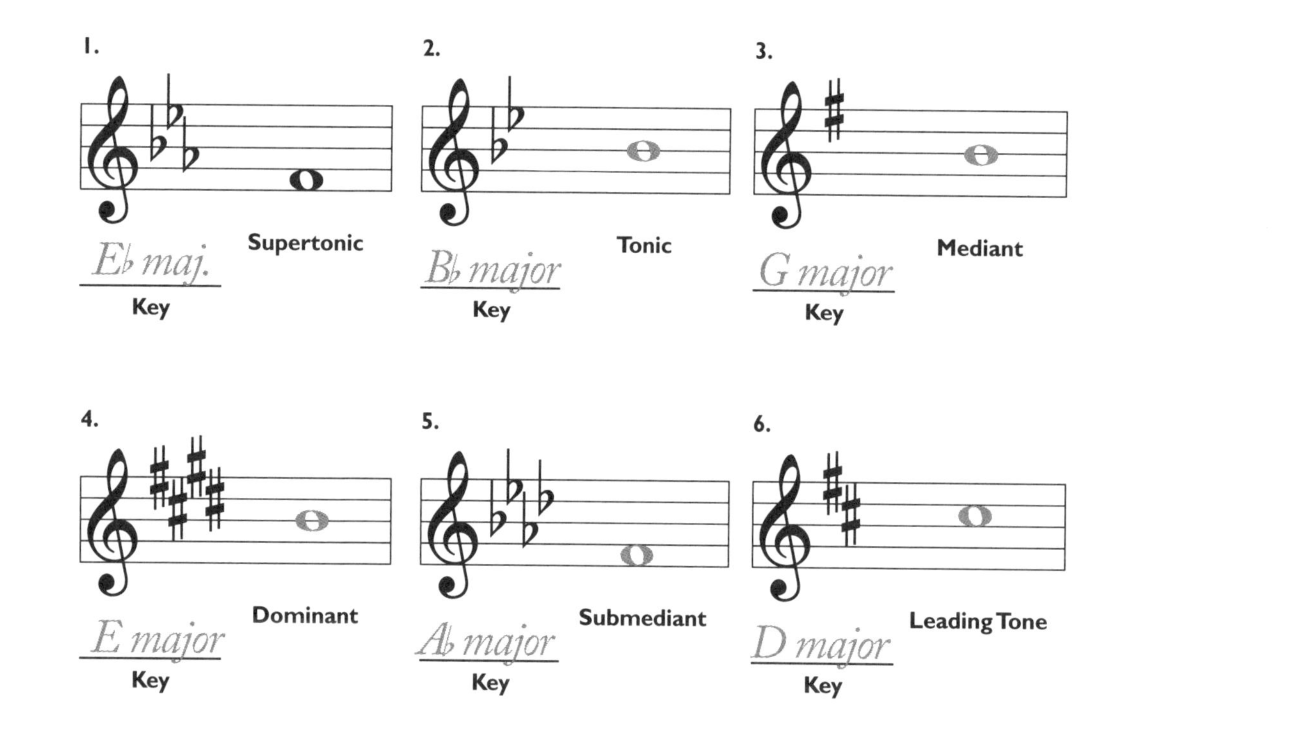

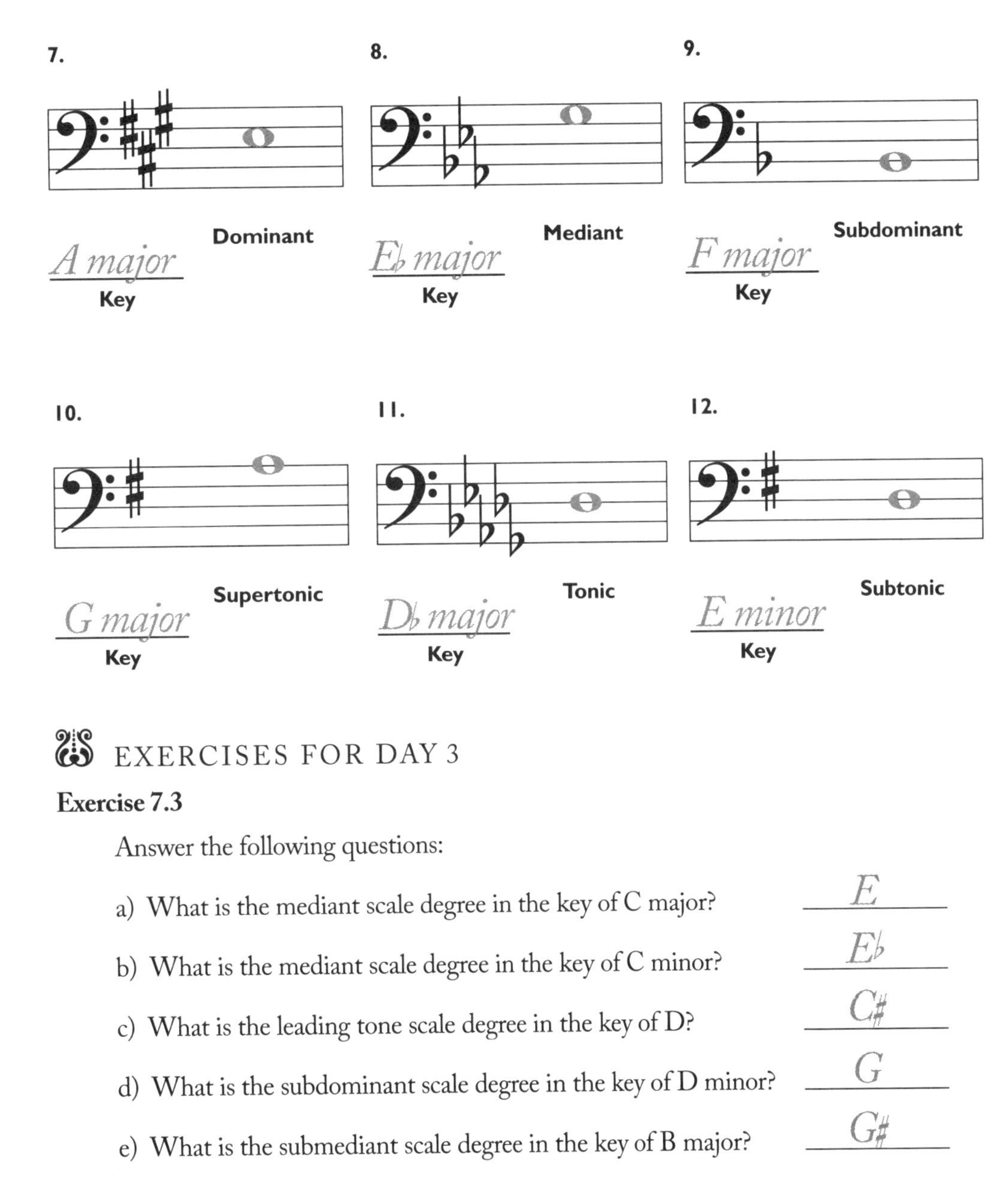

EXERCISES FOR DAY 3

Exercise 7.3

Answer the following questions:

a) What is the mediant scale degree in the key of C major? E

b) What is the mediant scale degree in the key of C minor? E♭

c) What is the leading tone scale degree in the key of D? C♯

d) What is the subdominant scale degree in the key of D minor? G

e) What is the submediant scale degree in the key of B major? G♯

Exercise 7.4

Use number transposition to transpose the following melodies into the indicated keys:

Transpose the melodies below into the key of G major.

1. Key of
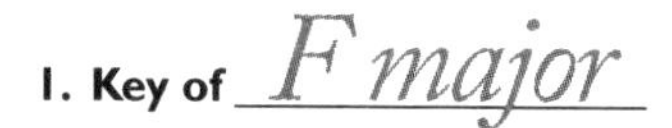

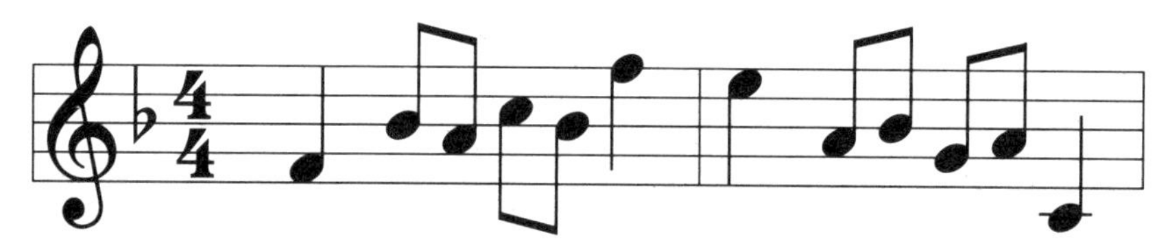

Key of G Major

2. Key of

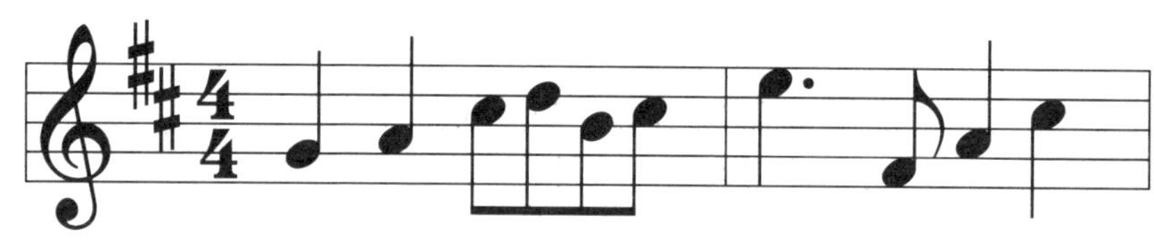

Key of G Major

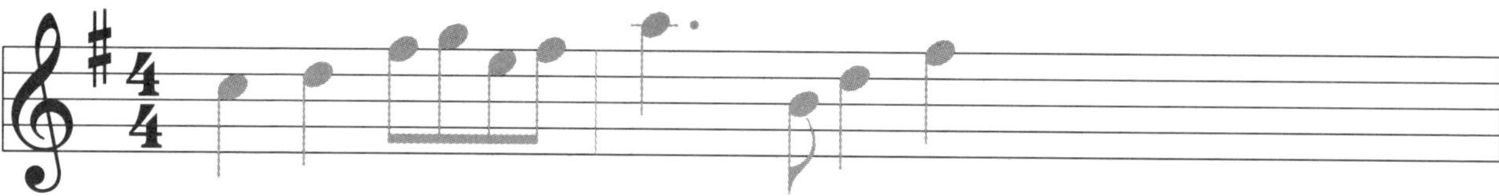

Using the blank staff below, compose a melody that fits the time signature.

3. Key of B♭ major

Each measure should contain notes whose values add up to four quarter notes.

Now transpose your melody above to the key of A major.

The first note of this melody should be one semitone down from the first note of the melody in the key of B♭ major above. The rest of the notes should contain the corresponding distance of the notes in the key of B♭ major.

EXERCISES FOR DAY 4

Exercise 7.5

Identify the correct scale degree name to the circled notes in the excerpt from "Be Thou My Vision."

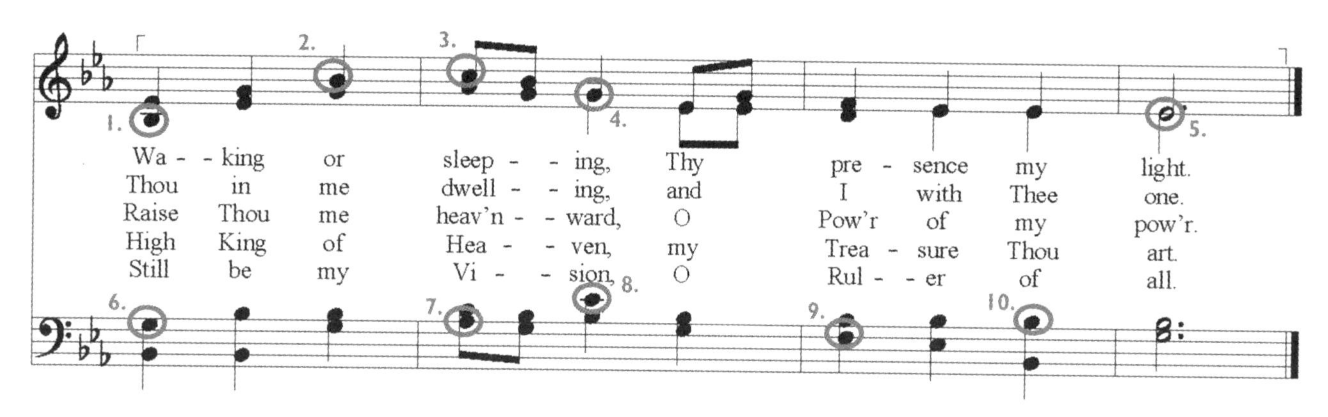

Key: *E♭ major*

1) *dominant*
2) *dominant*
3) *submediant*
4) *mediant*
5) *tonic*
6) *mediant*
7) *subdominant*
8) *tonic*
9) *supertonic*
10) *dominant*

Exercise 7.6

Use number transposition to transpose the first line of the hymn "There Is a Fountain Filled with Blood" into the key of D major. Use bar lines, clef signs, time signatures, and key signatures within your transposition.

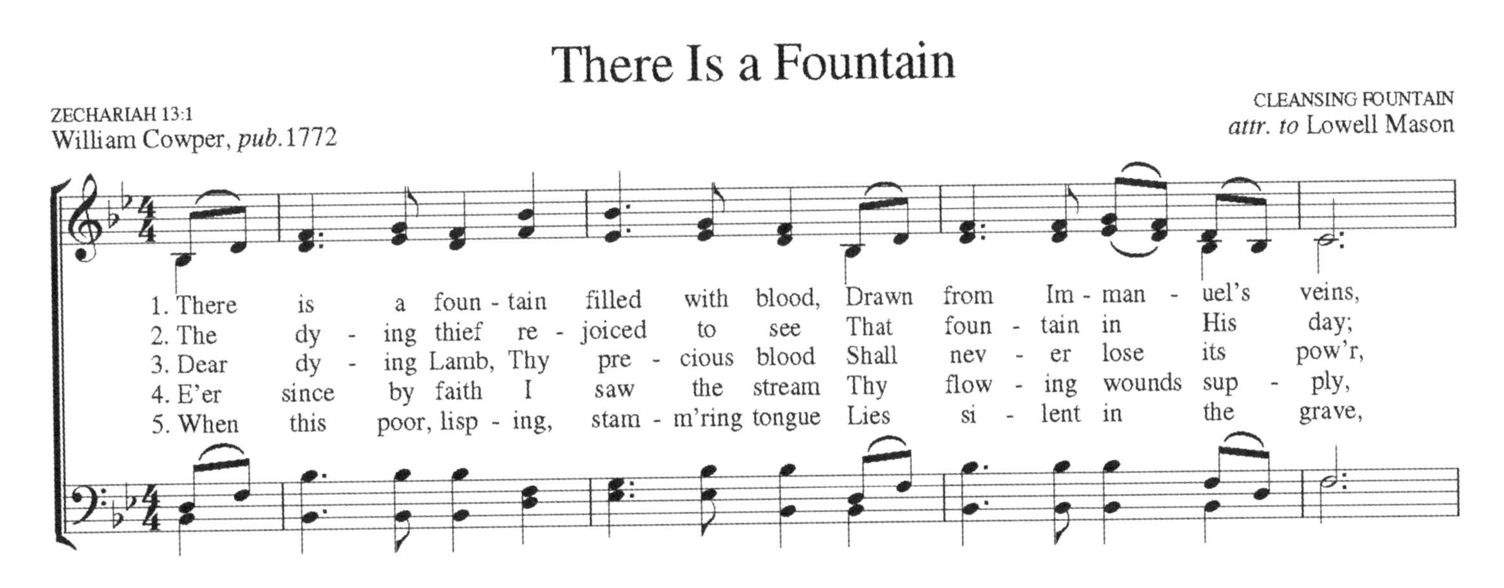

8 Intervals

Chapter 8 Review

Answer	Term
d	1. Interval
g	2. Harmonic interval
c	3. Melodic interval
e	4. Interval size
b	5. Interval quality
f	6. Augmented
l	7. Diminished
k	8. Simple interval
i	9. Compound interval
a	10. Major 6th
h	11. Minor 6th
n	12. Perfect 4th
m	13. Perfect 5th
j	14. Diminished 5th

a. C–A quality interval

b. The number of semitones in between two pitches

c. When one note occurs in succession of another note

d. The distance between two notes or two pitches

e. The number of steps the interval contains on the staff

f. To raise a note by one semitone

g. When two notes are played at the same time

h. E–C quality interval

i. Interval in a diatonic scale with a distance of more than eight notes

j. C–G♭ quality interval

k. Interval in a diatonic scale with a distance of eight notes or less

l. To lower a note by one semitone

m. F–C quality interval

n. C–F quality interval

Daily Exercises for Chapter 8

EXERCISES FOR DAY 1

Exercise 8.1

Read through the chapter and answer the following questions:

a) What is an interval? *An interval is the distance between two notes or two pitches.*

b) What is the difference between an interval size and interval quality?
Interval size is the number of steps the interval contains represented on the staff. Interval quality is the number of semitones between the two pitches.

c) Which interval sizes can be either major or minor?
second, third, sixth, and seventh

d) Which interval sizes can be perfect?
fourth, fifth, and eighth

e) What is the difference between harmonic and melodic intervals?
When two notes are played at the same time, it is called a harmonic interval. When one note occurs after another note, it is called a melodic interval.

f) What do augmented and diminished mean in the context of intervals?
Augmented means raised a semitone; diminished means lowered a semitone.

g) What is the difference between simple and compound intervals?
Intervals on a diatonic scale with a distance of eight notes (octave) or less between them are called simple intervals. Intervals in a diatonic scale with a distance of more than eight notes are called compound intervals.

h) List and explain the two ways of identifying the quality of an interval.
1. *Use the interval table and count semitones*
2. *Use the lower note of the interval as the tonic and establish the scale degree relationship*

Exercise 8.2

Use the measures below to answer the questions that follow.

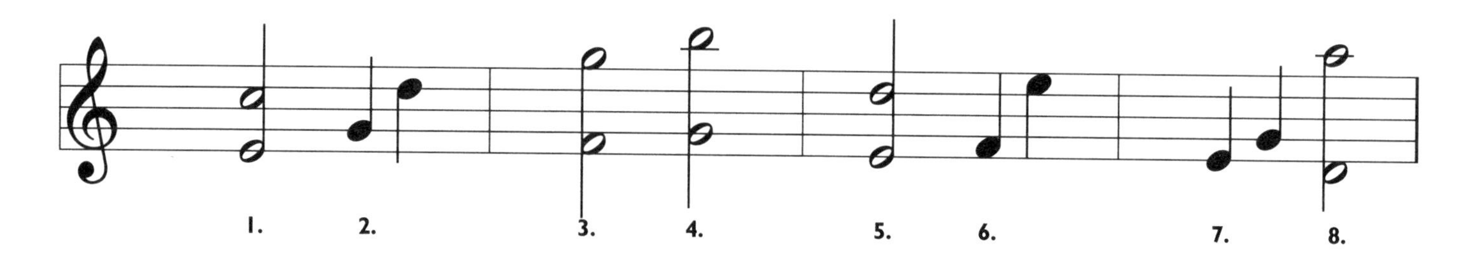

a) List the harmonic intervals in the measures above: 1, 3, 4, 5, 8

b) List the melodic intervals in the measures above: 2, 6, 7

c) List the harmonic intervals that are also simple intervals: 1, 5

d) List the harmonic intervals that are also compound intervals: 3, 4, 8

EXERCISES FOR DAY 2

Exercise 8.3

Intervals of size: Identify the following intervals below with the correct interval of size. Remember to ignore any accidentals. Accidentals do not affect the size of an interval.

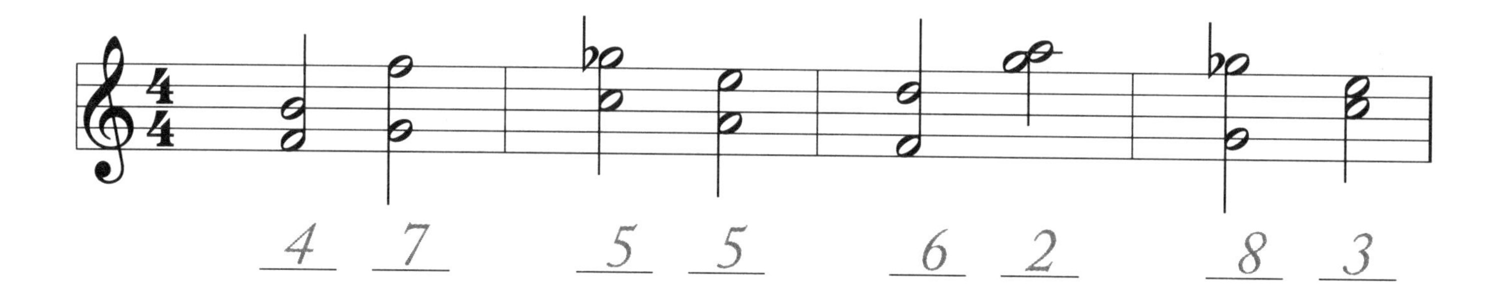

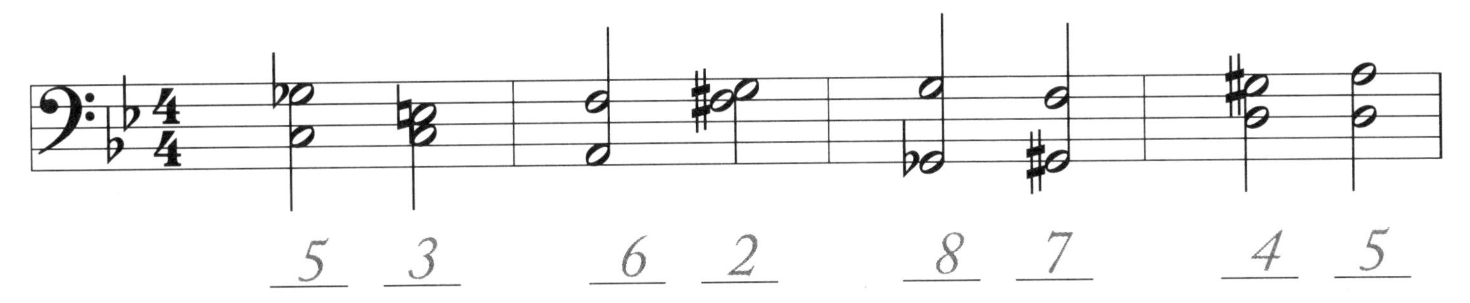

Exercise 8.4

Intervals of quality: Identify the following intervals as either minor or major second intervals. If needed, use your interval table. Do not forget to apply key signature before you identify.

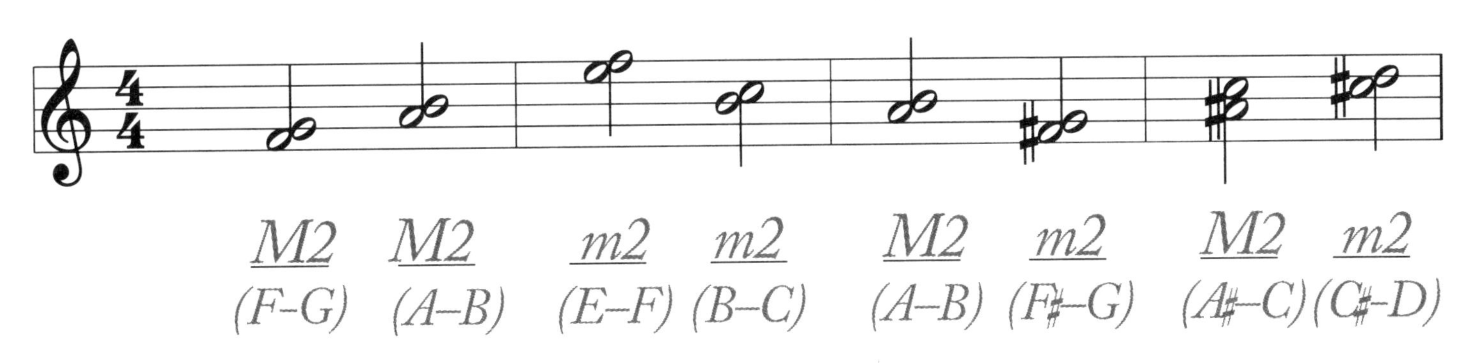

Like the major scale, the minor scale also consists of natural intervals of either major or minor second intervals. Can you label the quality of second intervals for the minor scale below? What is the minor scale below? B minor

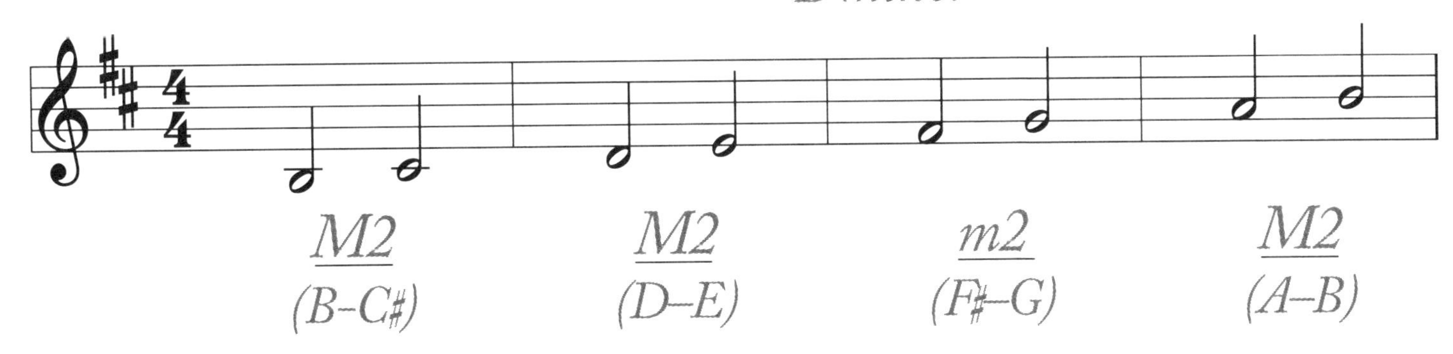

EXERCISES FOR DAY 3

Exercise 8.5

Identify the following intervals as either minor or major third intervals. If needed, use your interval table. Do not forget to apply key signature before you identify.

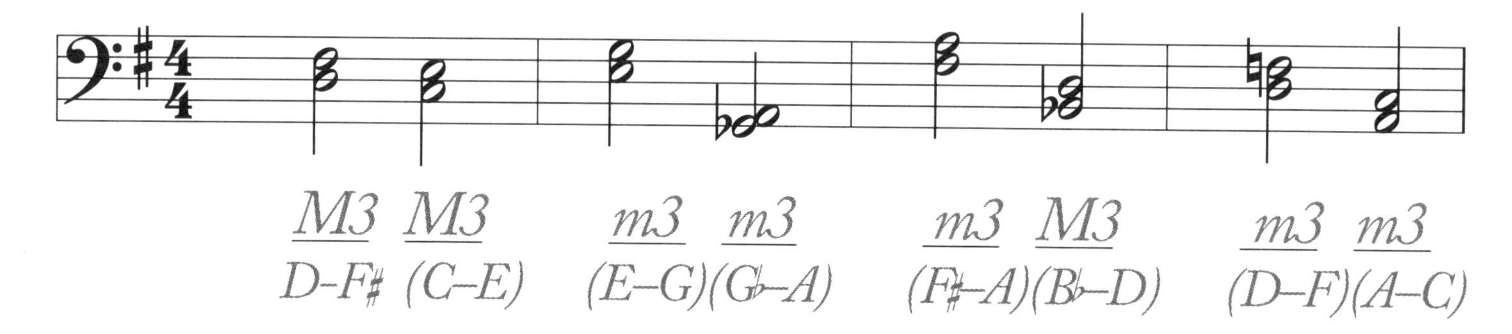

Identify the following intervals as either minor or major sixth intervals. If needed, use your interval table. Do not forget to apply key signature before you identify.

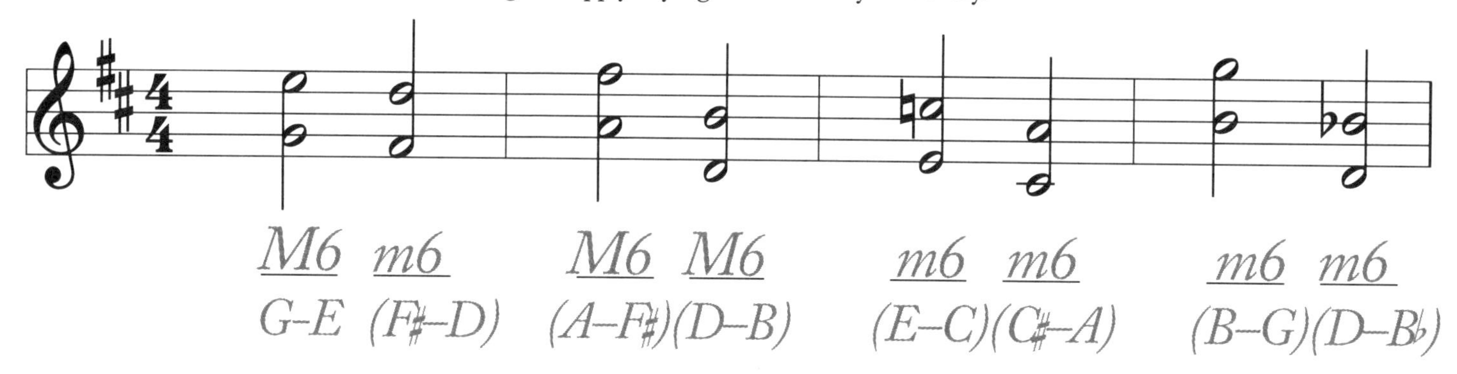

Identify the following intervals as either minor or major seventh intervals. If needed, use your interval table. Do not forget to apply key signature before you identify.

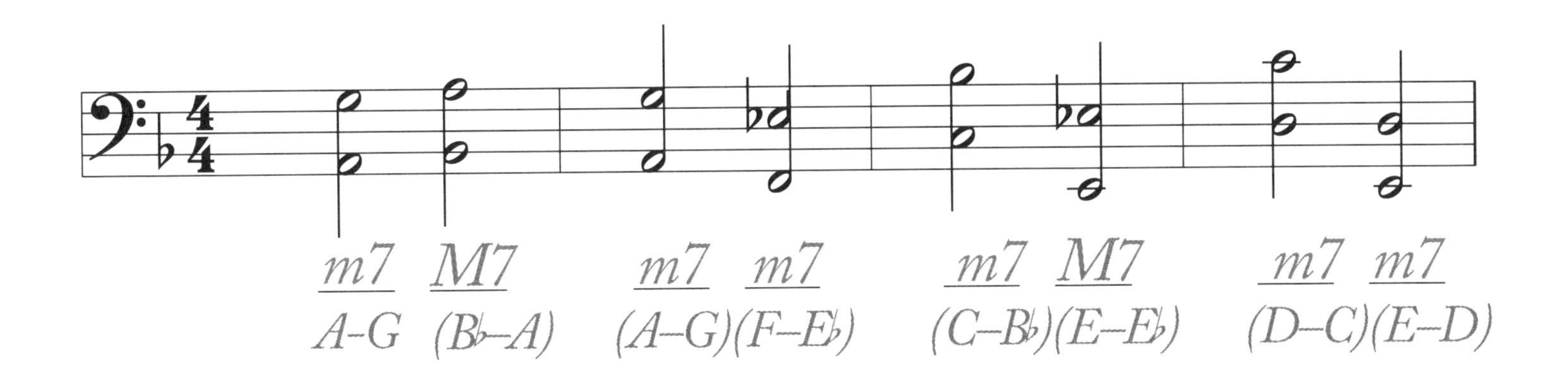

Identify the following intervals as either perfect fifths (P5) or fourths (P4) or octaves (P8). If needed, use your interval table. Do not forget to apply key signature before you identify.

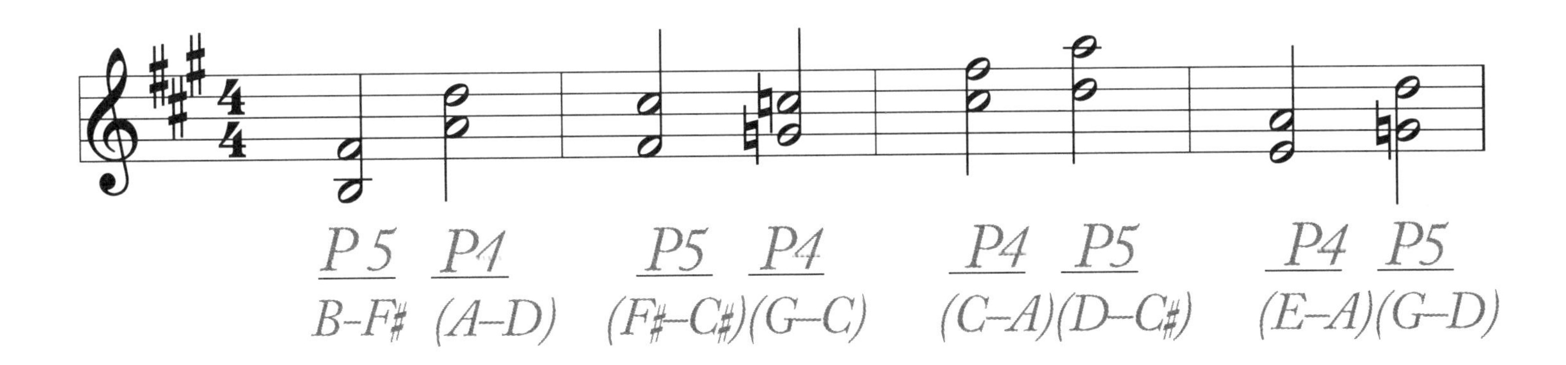

EXERCISES FOR DAY 4

Exercise 8.6

Notate the indicated harmonic intervals on the staves below. Remember, key signatures are important.

Refer to the Interval Table (Figure 8.10) to check answers.

P4th P5th m3rd M3rd m2nd M3rd M6th m3rd

M2nd P4th M3rd M6th M2nd octave P5th M7th

Exercise 8.7

Identify the following melodic intervals below by quality.

Tip: melodic intervals moving down will have the same number of semintones or whole steps as melodic intervals moving up. It may help to start with the lowest note in the interval to give the correct interval name.

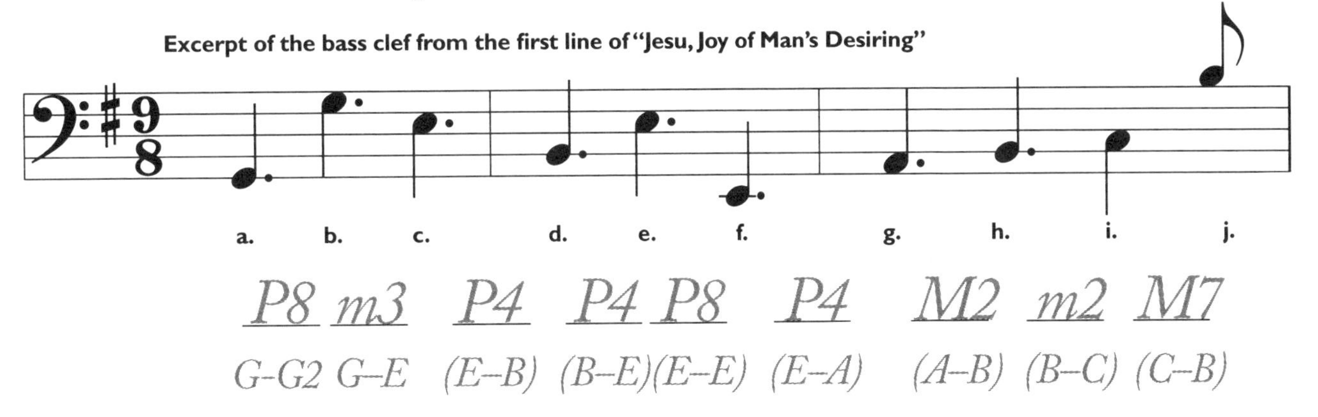

Give the scale degree name for each note of the bass line in the piece above.

a) *tonic (G)*

b) *tonic*

c) *submediant*

d) *mediant*

e) *submediant*

f) *submediant*

g) *supertonic*

h) *mediant*

i) *subdominant*

j) *mediant*

Triads and Triad Qualities

Chapter 9 Review

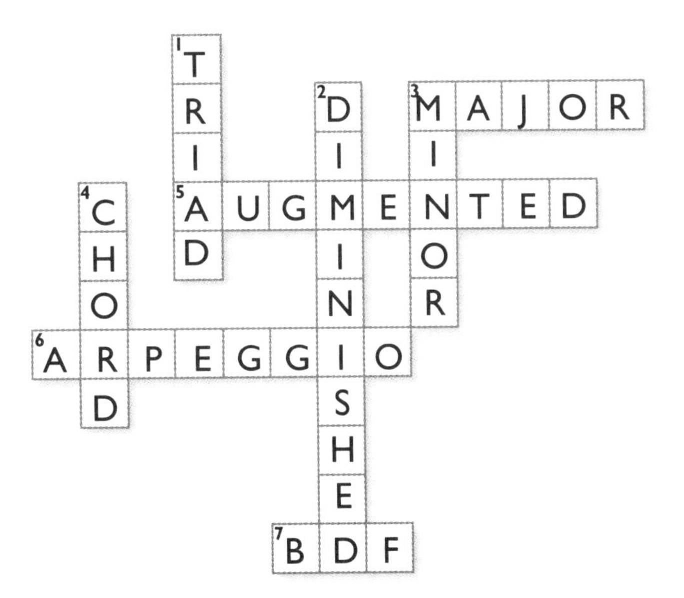

Daily Exercises for Chapter 9

EXERCISES FOR DAY 1

Exercise 9.1

Read through the chapter and answer the following questions:

a) What is the difference between a chord and a triad?

A triad is formed with three notes, consisting of the root, a third from the root, and a fifth from the root. A chord is any combination of notes played together.

b) What is an arpeggio?

When the notes of a chord are broken up and played in sequence, they are called an arpeggio.

c) What are the four qualities of triads?

Major, minor, augmented, and diminished

d) Give the symbols of the four qualities of triads. Use G as the root in your examples.

G (major), Gm (minor), G+ (augmented), G° (diminished)

e) Give the qualities of the intervals included in a major triad.

major third and perfect fifth

f) Give the qualities of the intervals included in a minor triad.

minor third and perfect fifth

Exercise 9.2

Supply the missing note in each triad to complete each of the triads below. Pay close attention to the major or minor quality indicated (no key signatures).

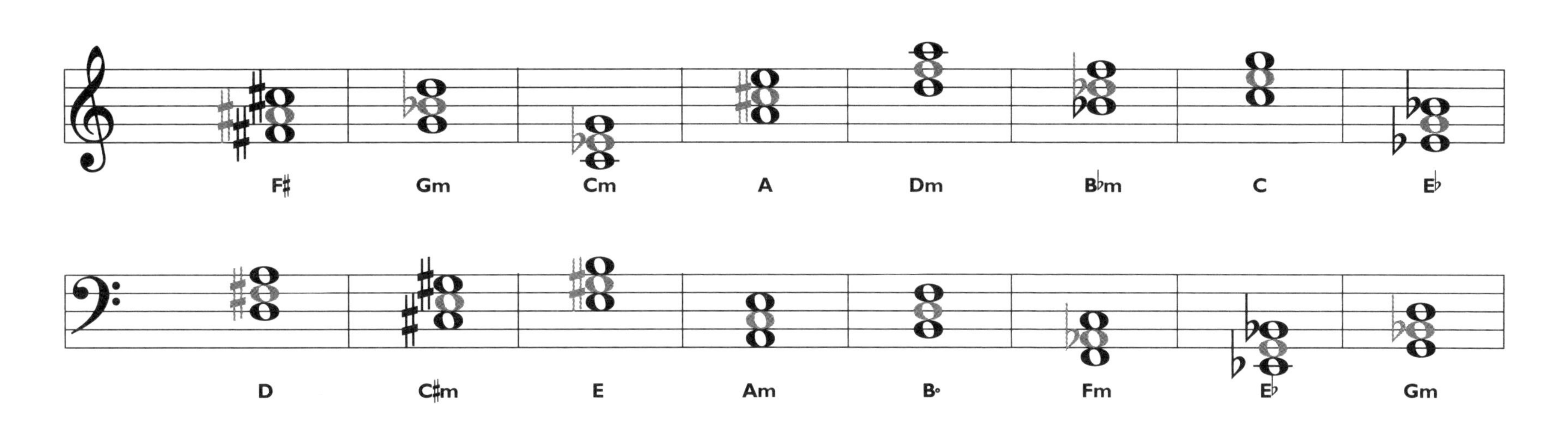

EXERCISES FOR DAY 2

Exercise 9.3

Supply the missing note in each triad to complete each of the triads below. Pay close attention to the major or minor quality indicated (no key signatures).

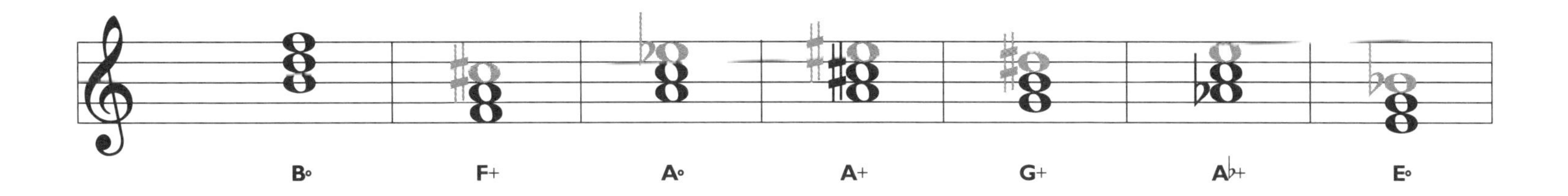

Exercise 9.4

Finish the indicated quality triads below.

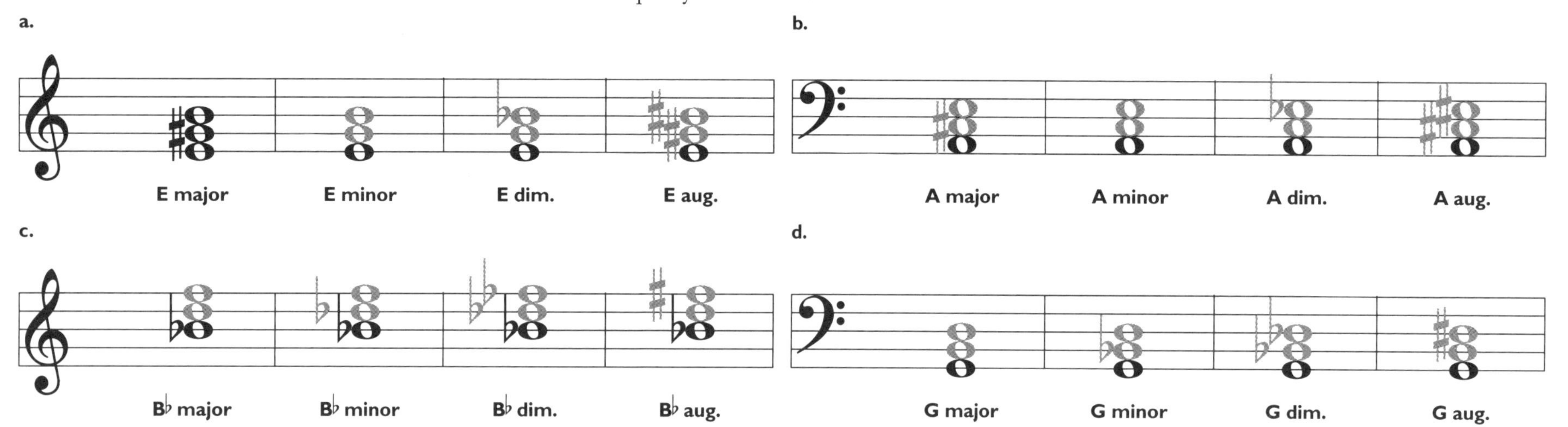

Exercise 9.5

Identify the quality of the triads below as major, minor, diminished, or augmented by the correct chord symbol.

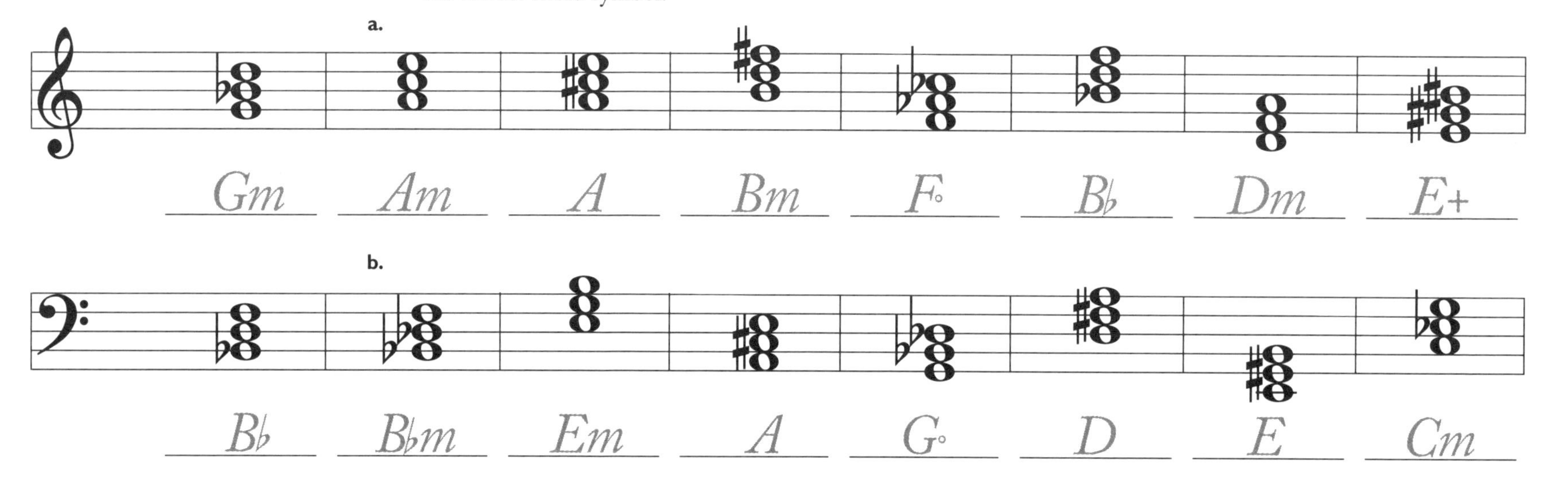

EXERCISES FOR DAY 3

Exercise 9.7

Correctly add accidentals to complete the requested qualities of the triads below.

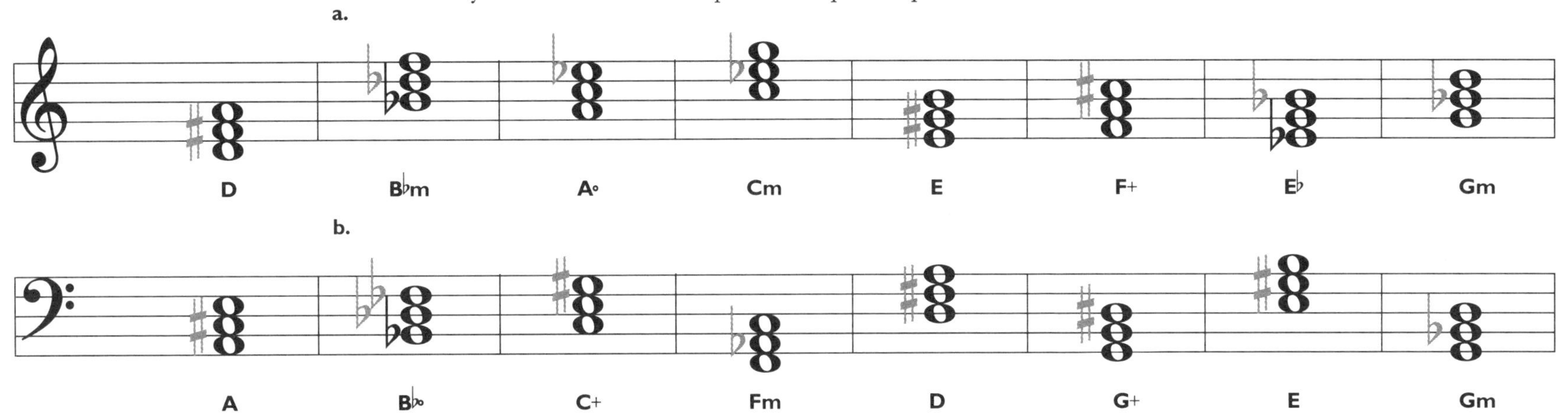

Exercise 9.8

Supply the missing notes to complete each of the triads below. Pay close attention to the major or minor quality indicated (no key signatures).

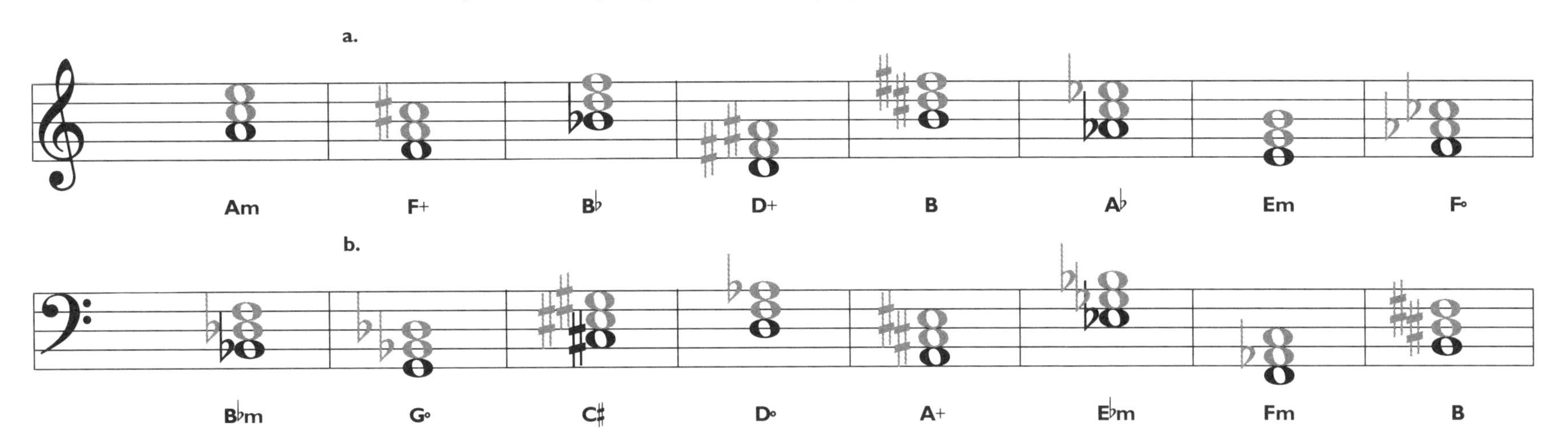

EXERCISES FOR DAY 4

Exercise 9.9

Supply the missing notes to complete each of the triads below. Pay close attention to the major or minor quality indicated (no key signatures).

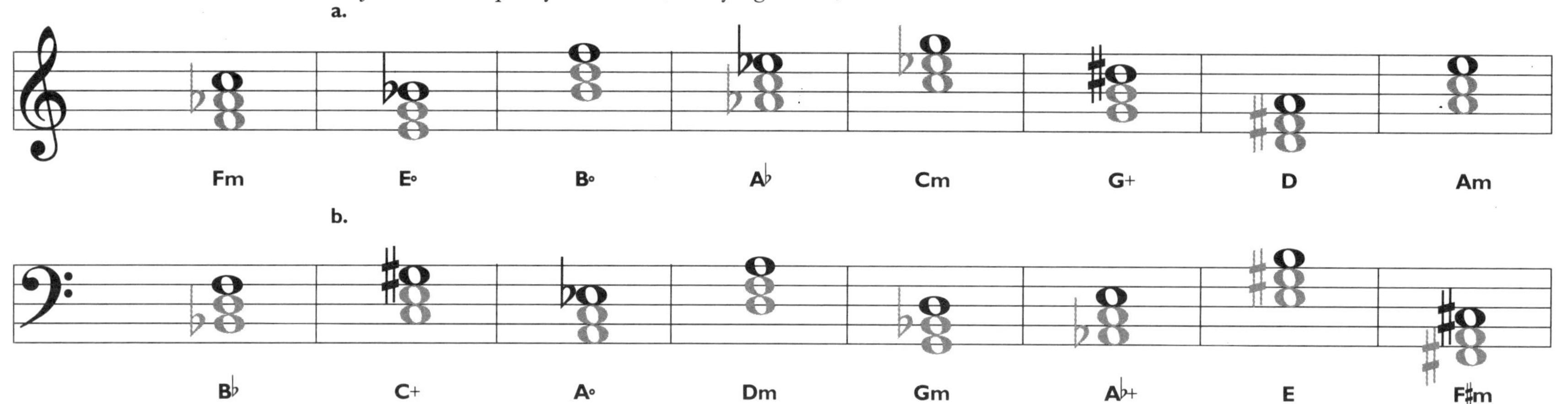

Exercise 9.10

Supply the missing notes to complete each of the triads below. For each triad, you are given a note, its interval name within the triad, and the triad quality. The first one is done for you.

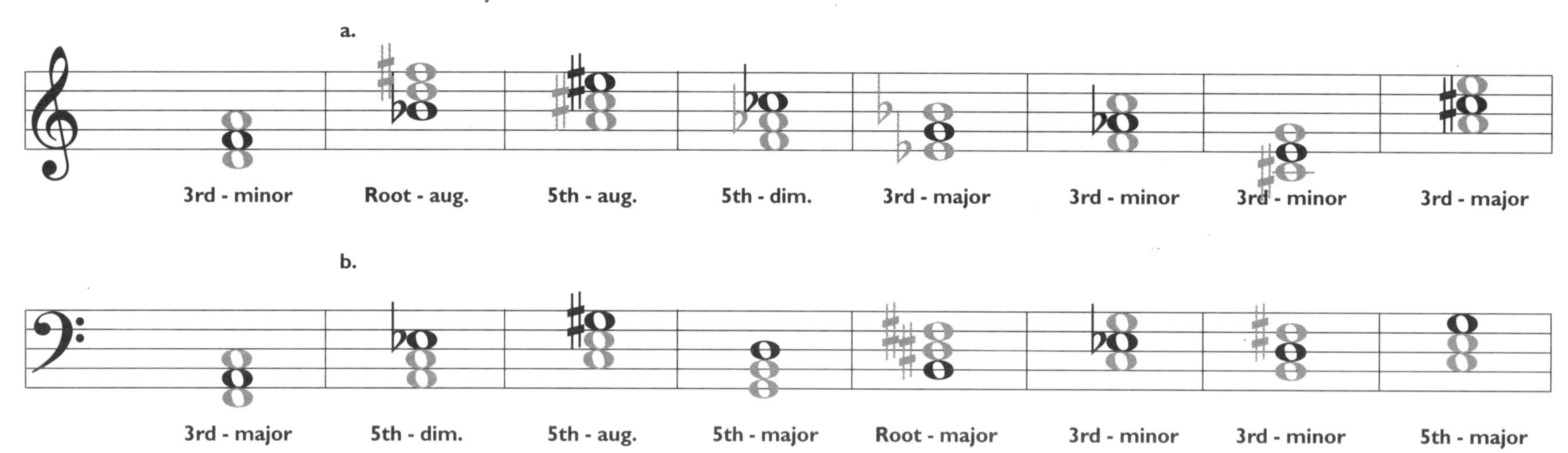

10 Triads: Roman Numeral Analysis

Chapter 10 Review

Refer to figures 10.6 and 10.7 to fill in the correct answers below.

h 1. ii
a 2. vi
j 3. III
n 4. V
c 5. iii
i 6. VI
e 7. IV
m 8. I
f 9. v
d 10. VII
k 11. vii°
g 12. ii°
l 13. i
b 14. iv

a. Submediant in major
b. Subdominant in minor
c. Mediant in major
d. Subtonic
e. Subdominant in major
f. Dominant in minor
g. Supertonic in minor
h. Supertonic in major
i. Submediant in minor
j. Mediant in minor
k. Leading tone
l. Tonic in minor
m. Tonic in major
n. Dominant in major

Daily Exercises for Chapter 10

EXERCISES FOR DAY 1

Exercise 10.1

Read through the chapter and answer the following questions:

a) What is Roman numeral analysis?

The naming of triads or chords in a given score using Roman numerals

b) What are diatonic triads?

Triads whose roots are built on the notes of a scale

c) Why is analysis with Roman numerals helpful?

a. Roman numerals are used to communicate scale degree numbers and scale degree names.

b. Roman numerals are used to communicate the quality of the triad.

c. Roman numerals can be easily adjusted to communicate notes or chords outside the key (accidentals).

d) Give an example of an arpeggiated triad below including a key signature and a bass or treble clef.

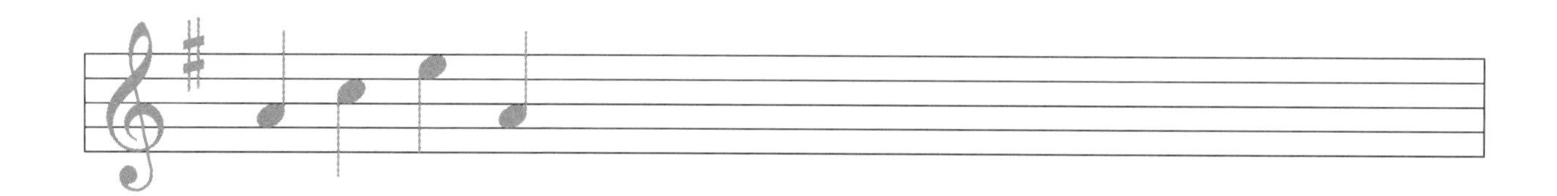

Exercise 10.2

Label the triads below with the correct triad degrees, making sure to note the key signatures.

a.

tonic *dominant*

b.

dominant *leading tone*

c.

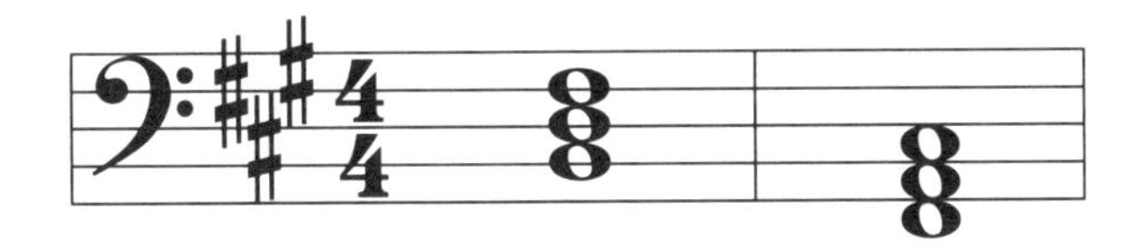

supertonic *submediant*

d.

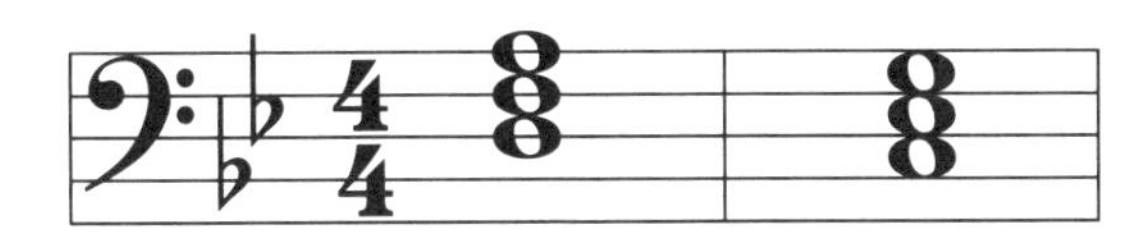

mediant *supertonic*

EXERCISES FOR DAY 2

Exercise 10.3

Give the corresponding Roman numeral including quality for the triad degrees below.

Major Key

a) Supertonic: ii b) Dominant: V c) Submediant: vi

d) Leading Tone: vii° e) Mediant: iii f) Subdominant: IV

Minor Key

a) Supertonic: ii° b) Dominant: v c) Submediant: VI

d) Subtonic: VII e) Mediant: III f) Subdominant: iv

Exercise 10.4

Use Roman numerals to identify the triads in the indicated **major** keys.

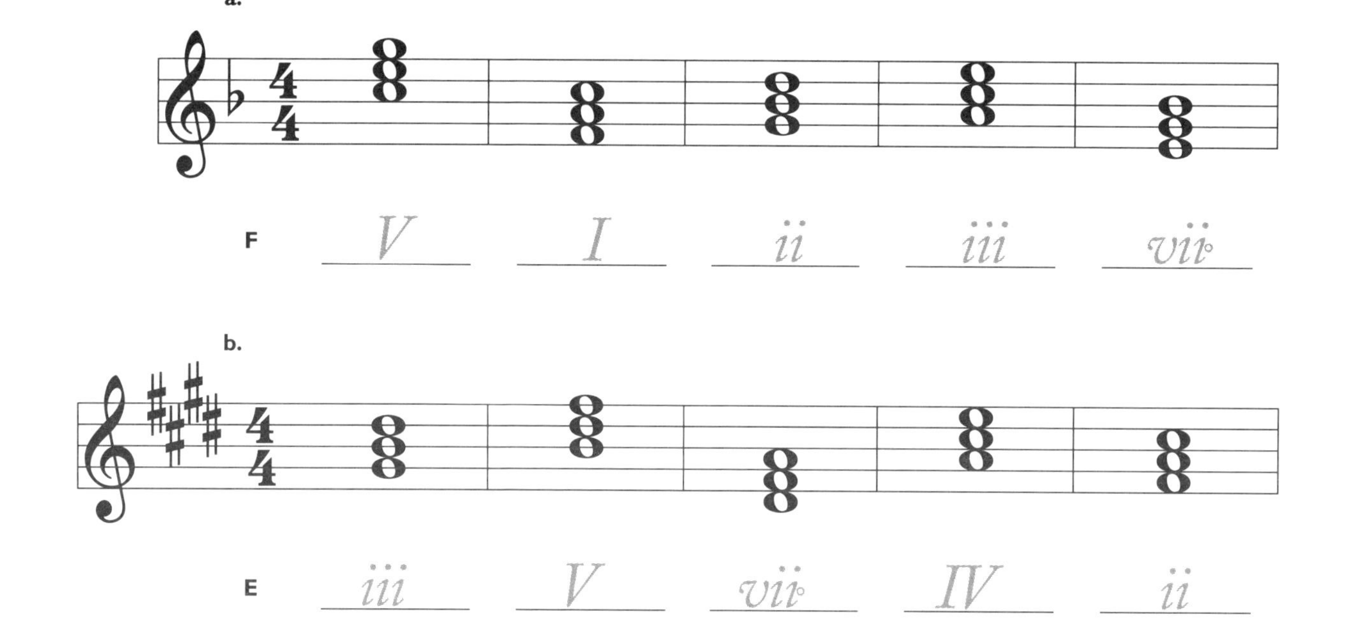

EXERCISES FOR DAY 3

Exercise 10.5

Use Roman numerals to identify the triads in the indicated **minor** keys.

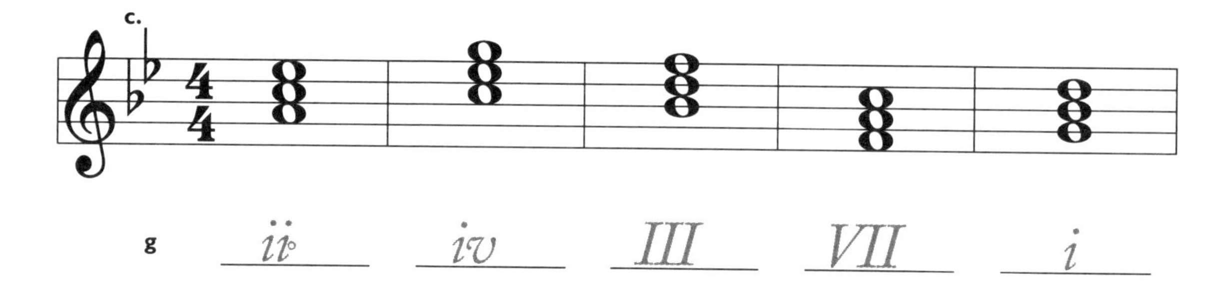

Exercise 10.6

You are given the major key and a Roman numeral indicating a specific triad. Write the correct triad in the staves below. Notice that key signatures are not written, so you will have to include accidentals in the staff to give the correct answer.

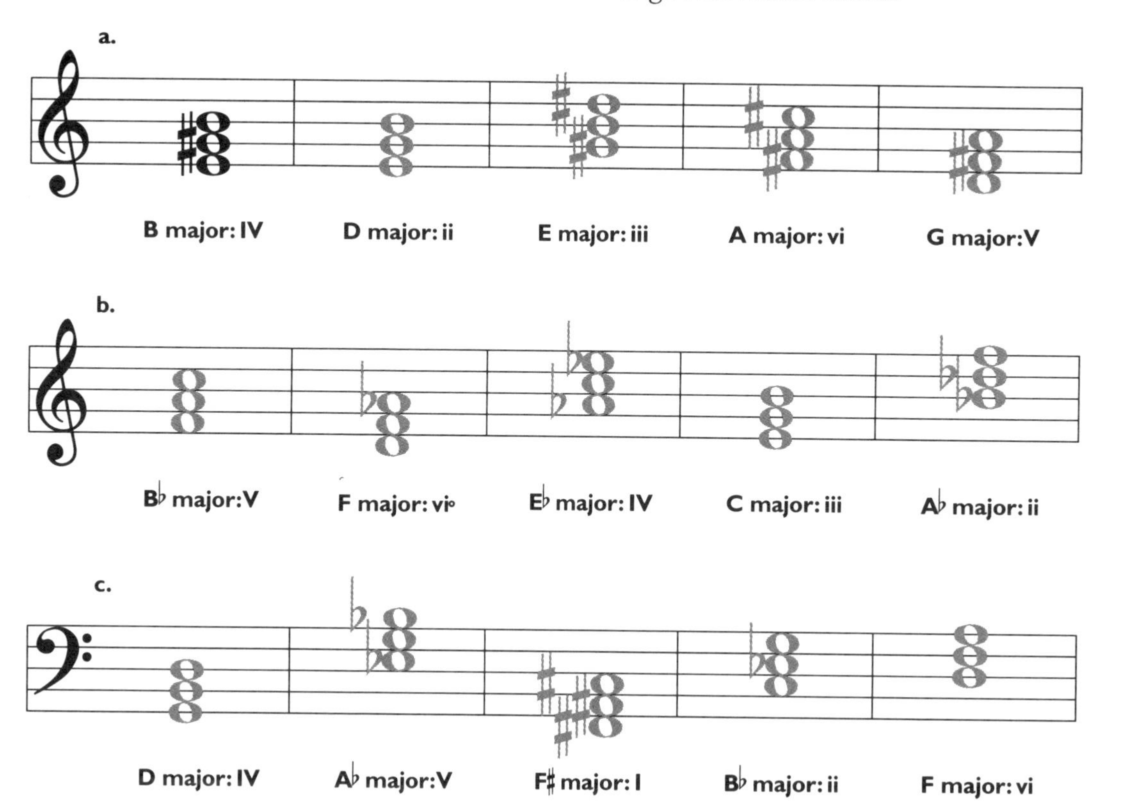

EXERCISES FOR DAY 4

Exercise 10.7

Use the Roman numeral analysis below to determine the key of each measure.

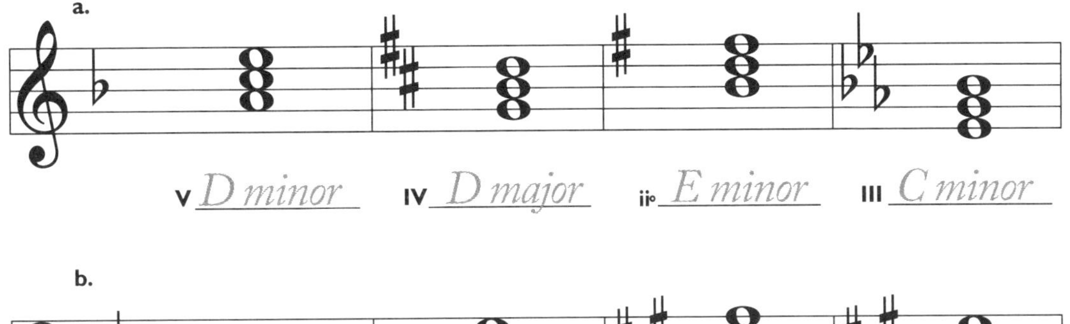

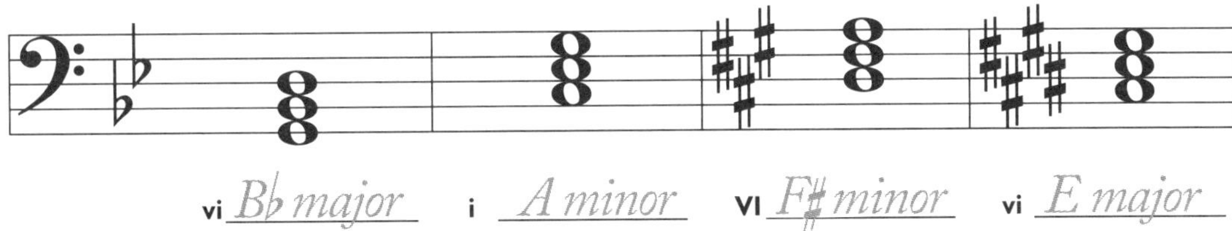

Exercise 10.8

Give Roman numeral analysis to the arpeggiated triads below. The keys are all major keys.

b.
vi
IV
iii
iii
ii
c.
vii°
vi
V
IV
I

11 Triad Inversions

Chapter 11 Review

N	O	I	S	R	E	V	N	I	D	N	O	C	E	S
F	I	R	S	T	I	N	V	E	R	S	I	O	N	Q
J	K	C	J	Y	N	R	N	T	T	W	R	R	R	J
J	F	D	X	D	N	X	D	Z	B	O	W	L	Z	Q
A	X	N	T	N	R	T	X	L	O	L	Z	L	T	R
B	M	T	J	X	N	Q	Y	T	D	B	E	Y	D	Z
J	M	T	B	J	V	W	P	B	V	F	P	B	V	V
T	V	R	L	Z	L	O	W	R	T	D	A	T	G	N
M	D	J	Z	C	S	L	Y	R	D	G	M	B	Y	Y
M	J	V	K	I	G	L	Q	M	B	B	G	Q	J	V
L	J	G	T	K	T	E	B	N	L	B	X	Q	B	T
Y	R	I	N	Y	N	W	Q	X	B	K	L	P	B	M
N	O	Y	X	P	N	Y	Y	Y	X	M	Y	M	L	V
N	P	D	M	D	T	B	B	Q	Z	L	T	L	K	P

Daily Exercises for Chapter 11

In these exercises for working with inversions, there will be no minor keys. All of the examples in your exercises will be major key signatures.

EXERCISES FOR DAY 1

Exercise 11.1

Rewrite the root position triads below into first and second inversion triads.

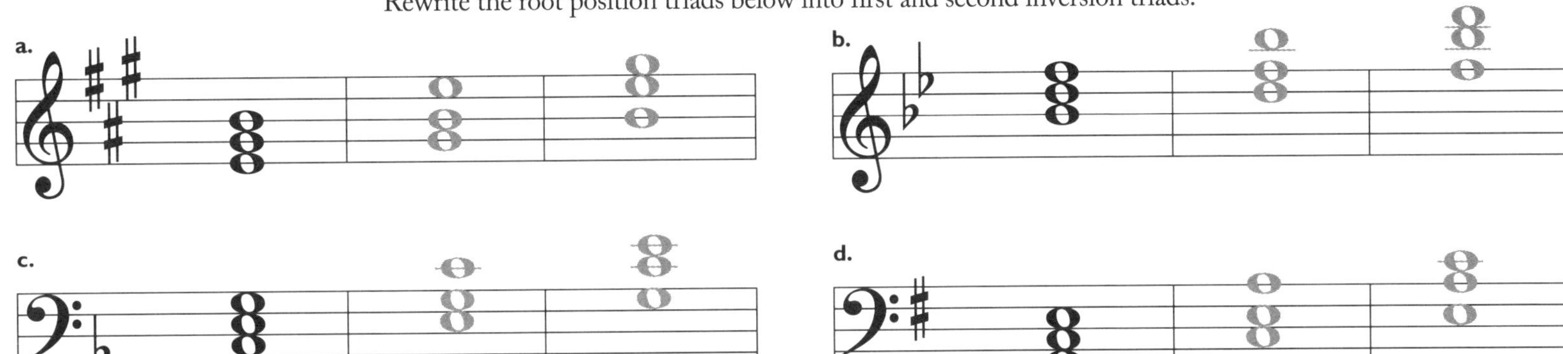

Rewrite the second inversion triads into root position triads.

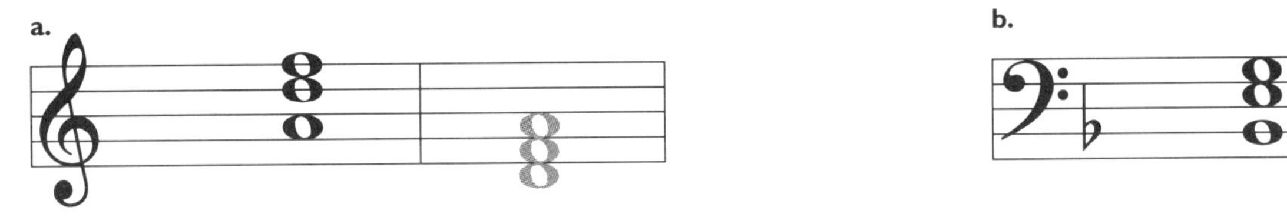

Exercise 11.2

Identify the following triads as root, first, or second inversions.

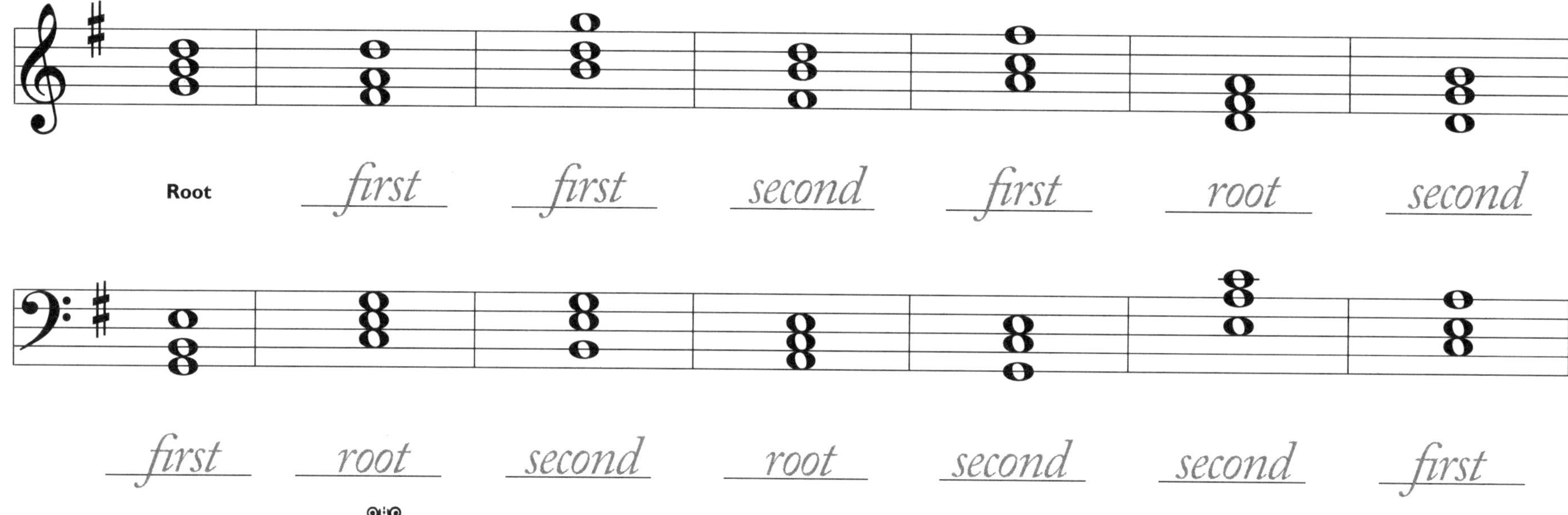

EXERCISES FOR DAY 2

Exercise 11.3

a) Label the triads below by letter and quality (use your keyboard sheet).

b) Label the triads below by triad degree.

c) Label the triads in Roman numeral analysis including inversion type.

a)	D minor	D minor	D minor	A dim	F major	C minor	B♭ major
b)	mediant	mediant	mediant	leading tone	dominant	supertonic	tonic
c)	iii^5_3	iii^6_4	iii^6	$vii^{\circ 5}_{3}$	V^6	ii^6	I^5_3

Exercise 11.5

Label the following triads in Roman numeral analysis indicating the type of inversion. Make sure you note the key signatures (use your keyboard sheet if you need to).

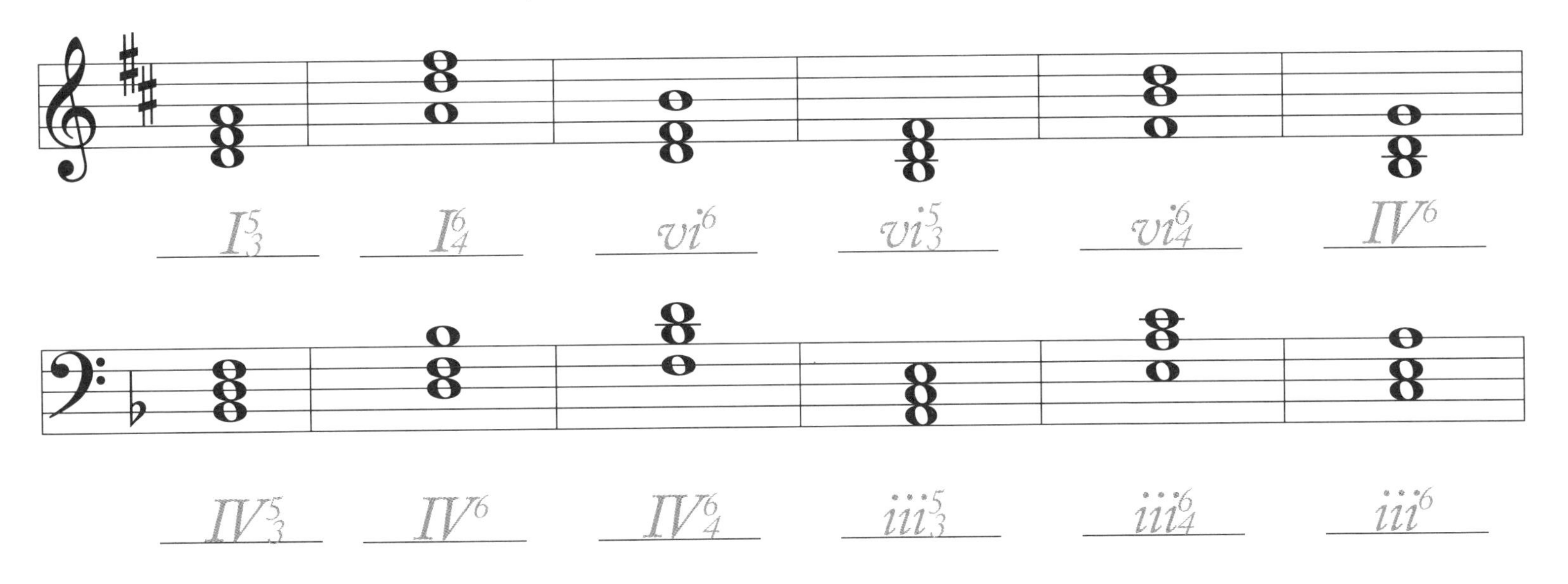

EXERCISES FOR DAY 3

Exercise 11.6

Rewrite the following augmented and diminished triads into first and second inversions.

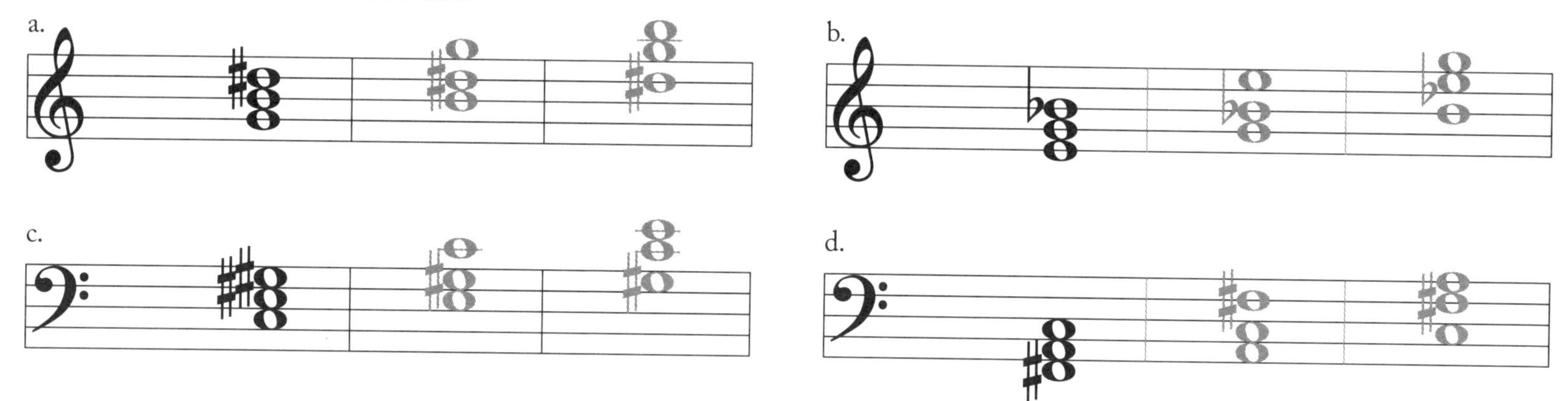

Label the following augmented or diminished triads below as either root, first inversion, or second inversion.

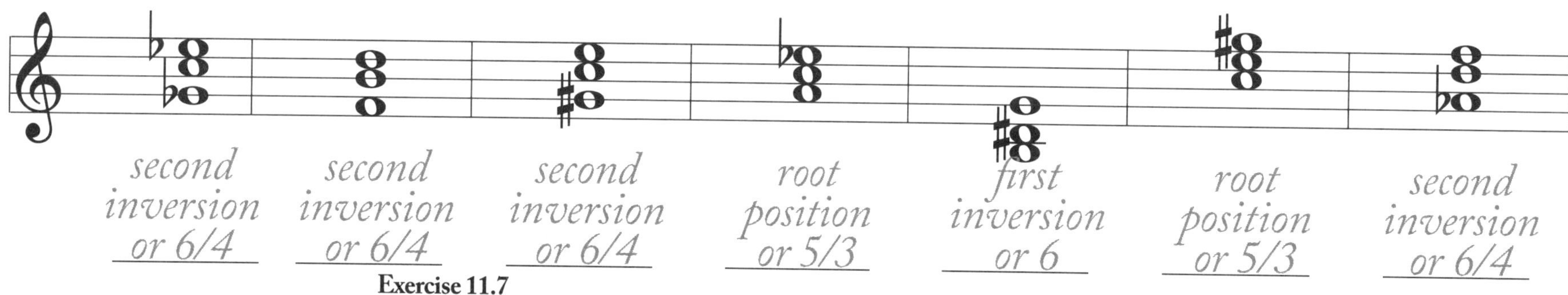

Exercise 11.7

Finish writing the triads indicated by the Roman numeral analysis. Remember the symbols for quality of triads. You WILL use accidentals on some answers.

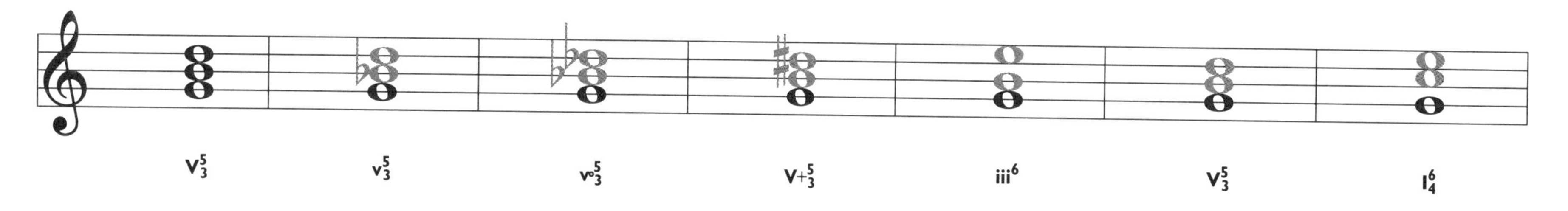

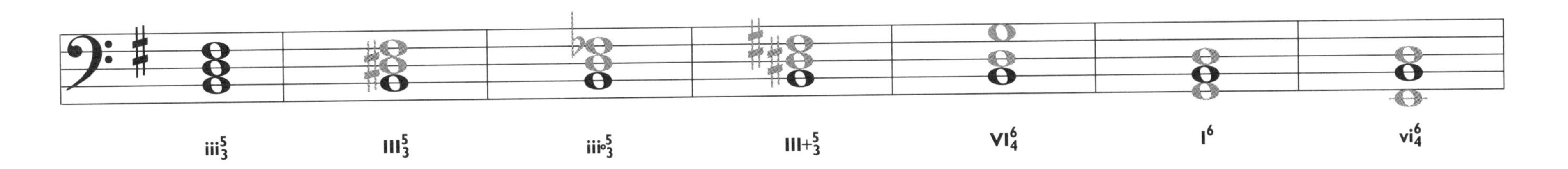

EXERCISES FOR DAY 4

Exercise 11.8

Label the following triads in Roman numeral analysis indicating the type of inversion. Make sure you note the key signature.

Exercise 11.9 Advanced Theory (Brain Teasers)

Build the specified triad above the given bass note. If the note does not contain an accidental, it is meant to be natural. The key signatures are not given nor needed. The types of inversions will indicate all you need to give the correct triad and quality. If there are no inversion number(s), it is a root position. Do not be frustrated; this exercise will take you some time. Use your keyboard sheet if needed. Write the name of each triad above the notated triad as noted in the examples below.

A = augmented dim = diminished m = minor M = major

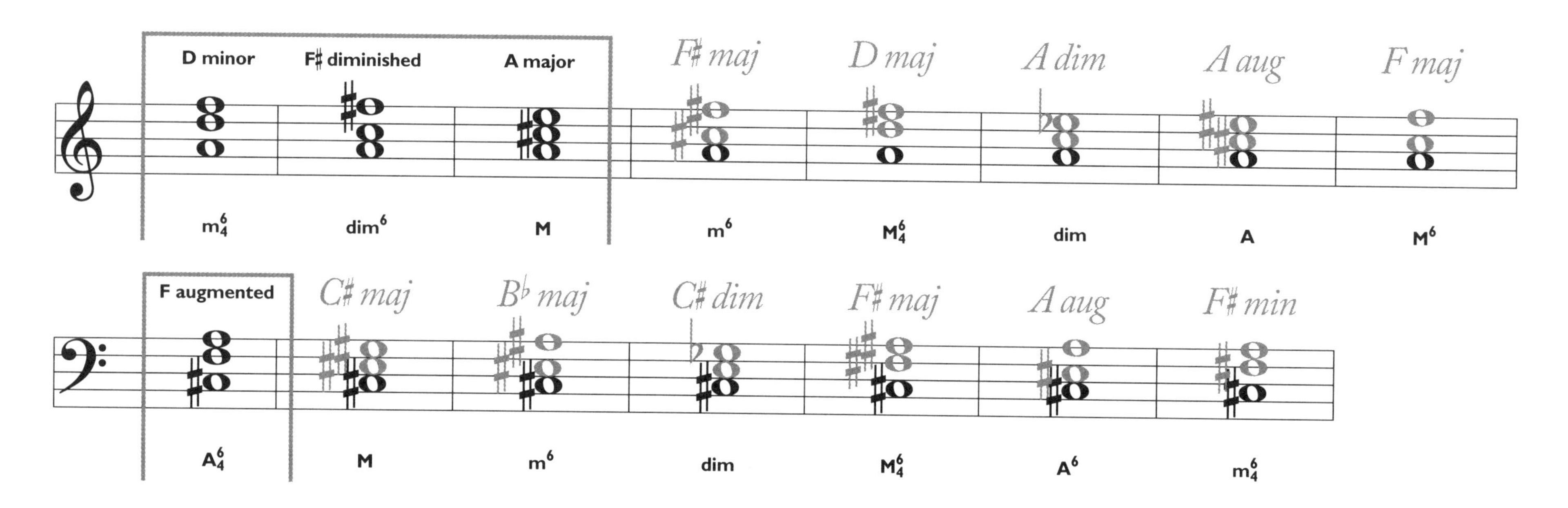

12 Score Analysis

Chapters 6–12 Review

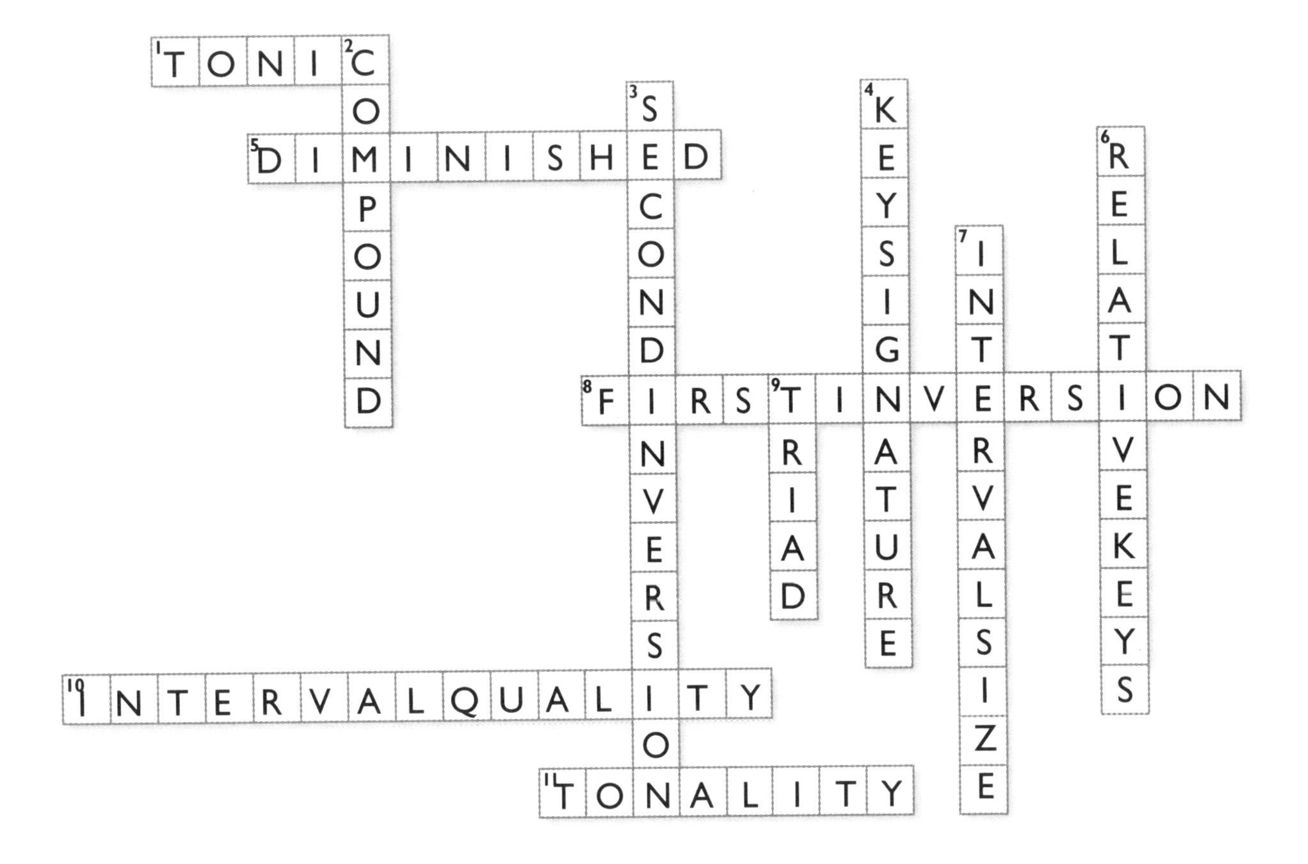

Daily Exercises for Chapter 12

EXERCISES FOR DAY 1

Exercise 12.1

Use both the bass and treble clefs to analyze the type of triad in the scores below (but do not yet write out the figured bass analysis). Write out the notes.

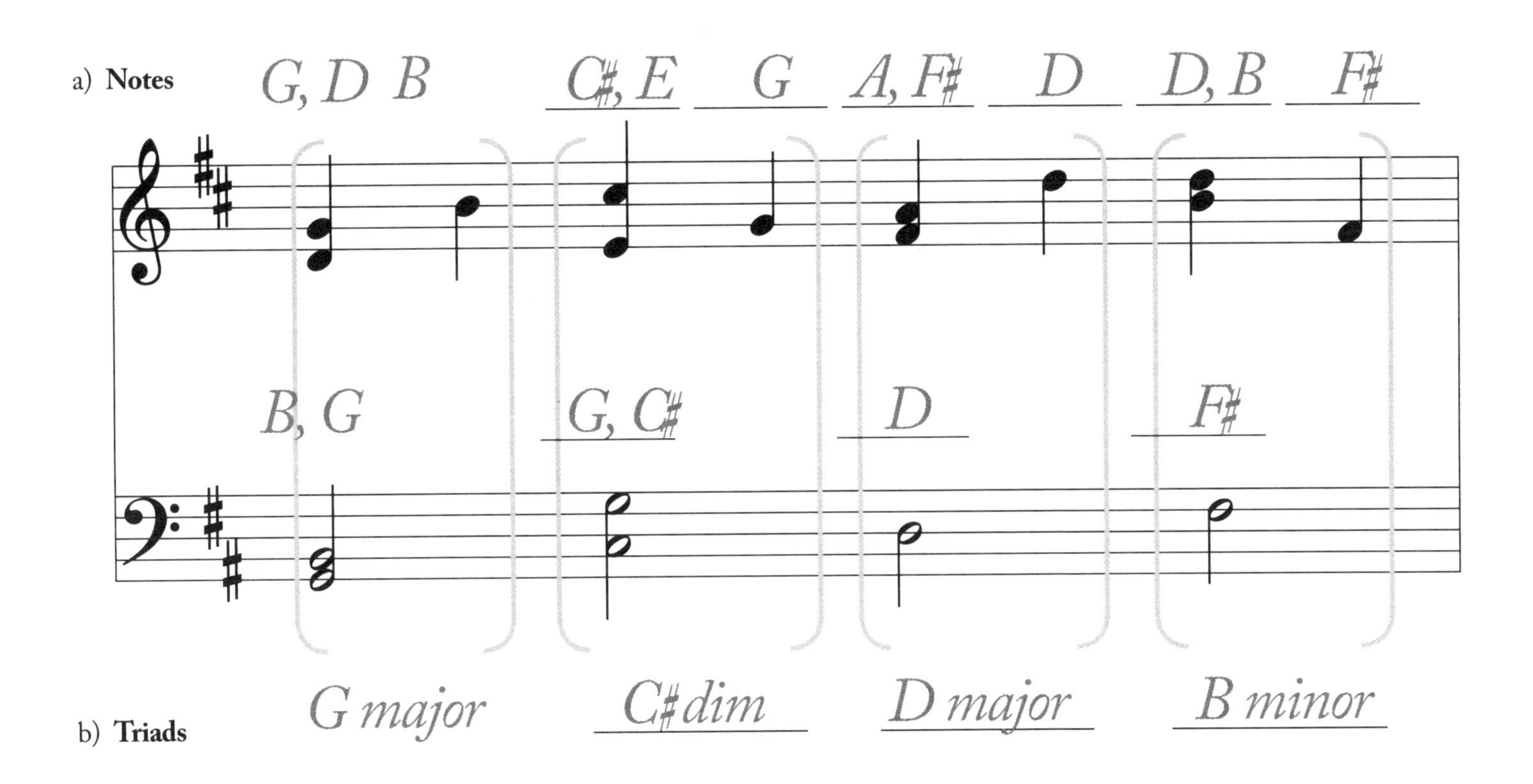

Exercise 12.2

Use the notes below to label the type of triad in each group of notes (e.g., G major).

1. *D minor*
2. *E♭ major*
3. *B♭ major*
4. *C minor*
5. *G minor*
6. *F major*
7. *A diminished*
8. *B♭ major*

EXERCISES FOR DAY 2

Exercise 12.3

Use the measures below to label the type of triad in each group of notes. Include the "extra" note in your answer. Duplicates are not "extra" notes. List the extra note next to the triad name.

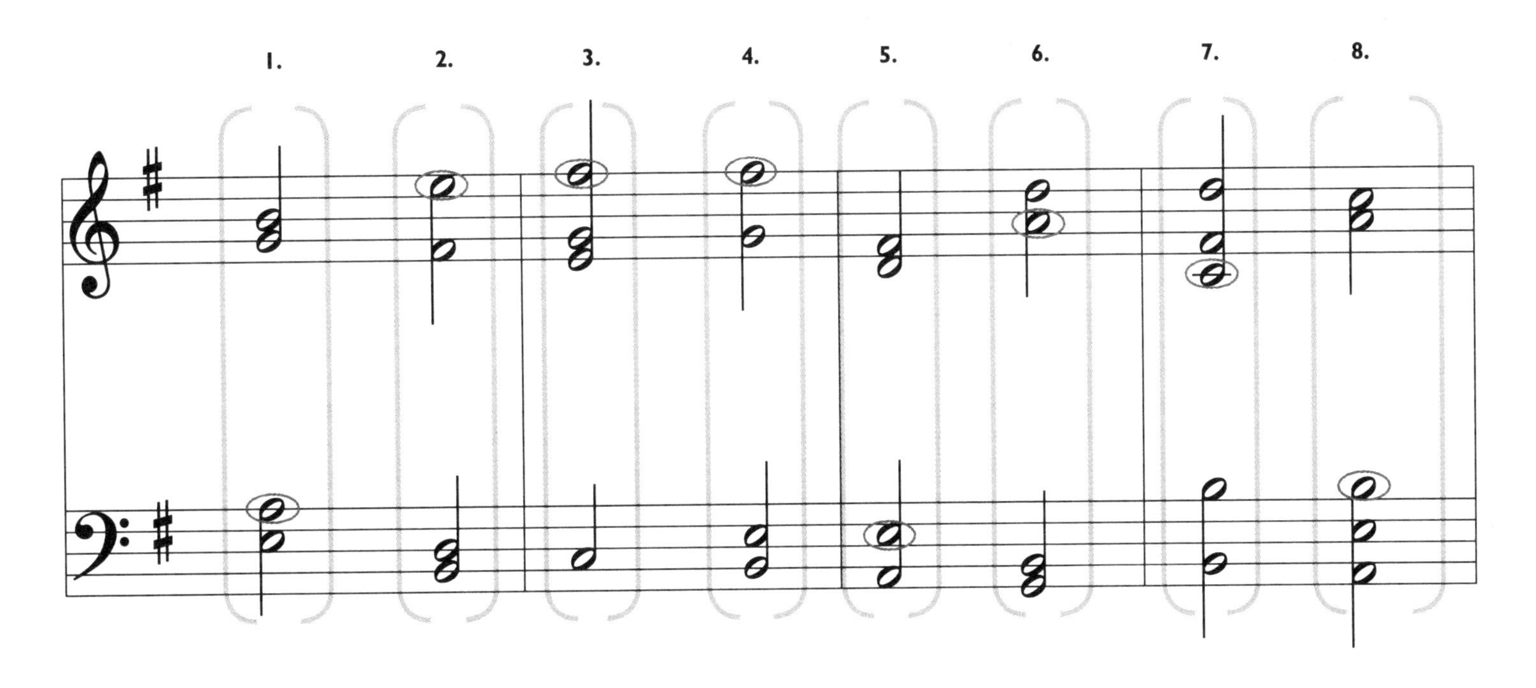

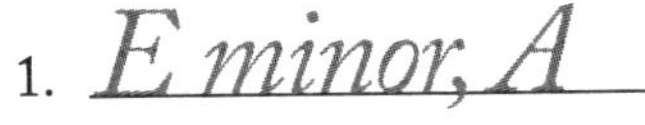

1. E minor, A
2. B minor, E
3. C major, F♯
4. E minor, F♯
5. D major, E
6. G major, A
7. B minor, C
8. A minor, B

Music is like a dream. One that I cannot hear.

—Ludwig van Beethoven

Exercise 12.4

Use the measures below to label the type of triad in each group of notes. Note that all of these groups of notes have implied notes. List the implied note next to the triad name.

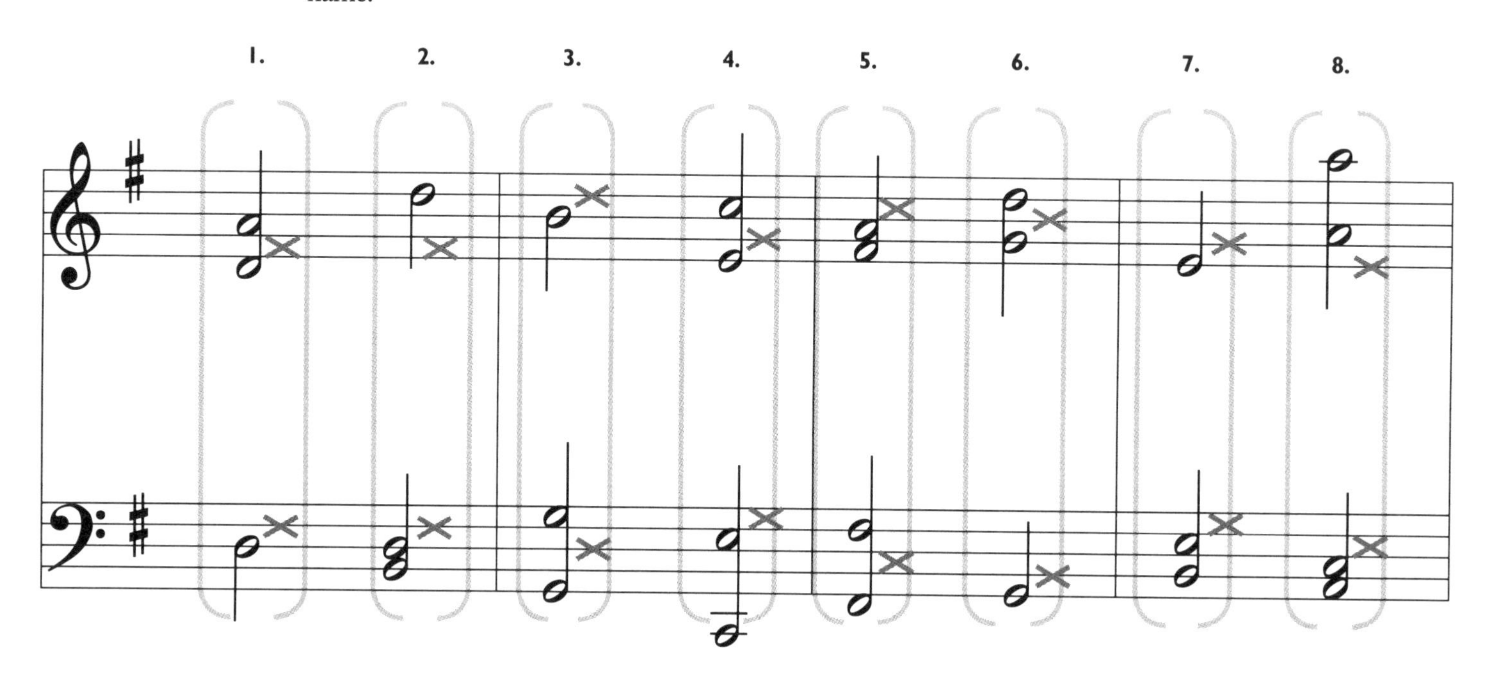

1. *D major, F♯*
2. *B minor, F♯*
3. *G major, D*
4. *C major, G*
5. *F♯ diminished, C*
6. *G major, B*
7. *E minor, G*
8. *A minor, E*

EXERCISES FOR DAY 3

Exercise 12.5

Use Roman numerals in your analysis for the groups of notes indicated below. Note the key and remember the symbols for major, minor, augmented, and diminished triads.

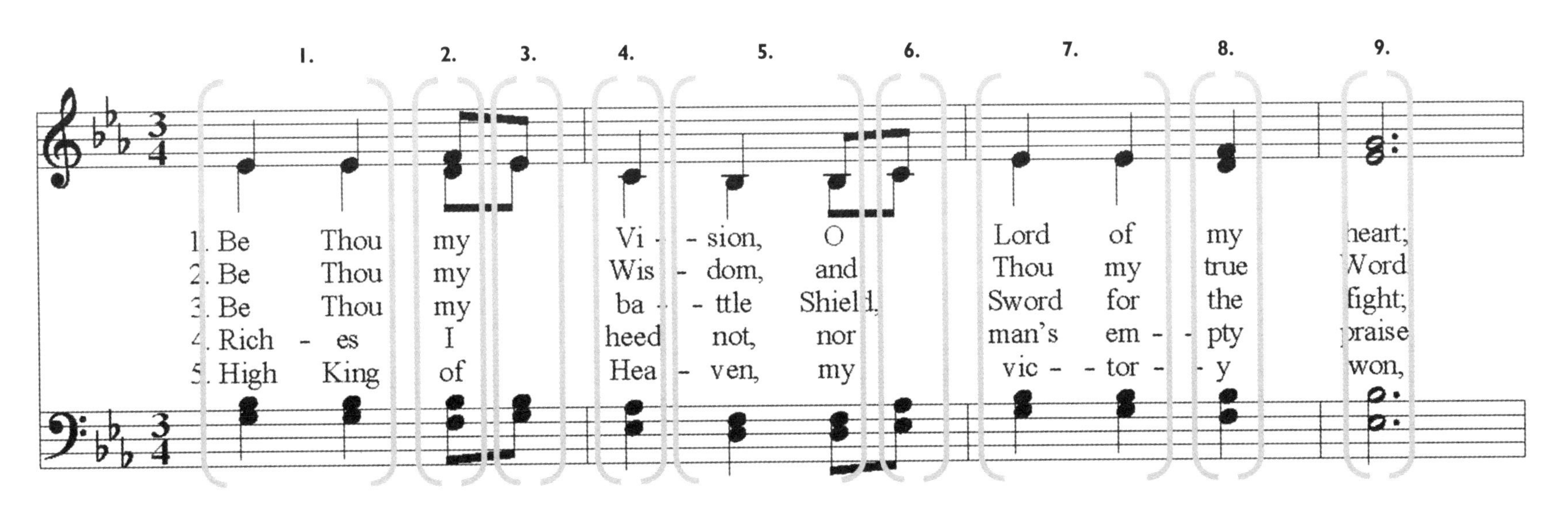

1. I
2. V
3. I
4. IV
5. V
6. IV
7. I
8. V
9. I

Exercise 12.6

Use Roman numerals in your analysis for the groups of notes indicated below in this excerpt of "There Is a Fountain Filled with Blood." There will be "extra" notes and you will have to use "implied" notes in this exercise. Give the best possible answer.

1. *I* 2. *I* 3. *ii with extra note E♭*

4. *IV* 5. *I* 6. *V for F major**

**The C note is in the triad F major and the F note is in the triad C minor. The correct answer here is determined by the lowest note—the F.*

EXERCISES FOR DAY 4

Exercise 12.7

Use figured bass for the score from "When I Survey the Wondrous Cross" below. The lowest note in each group of notes will help you determine the inversion type.

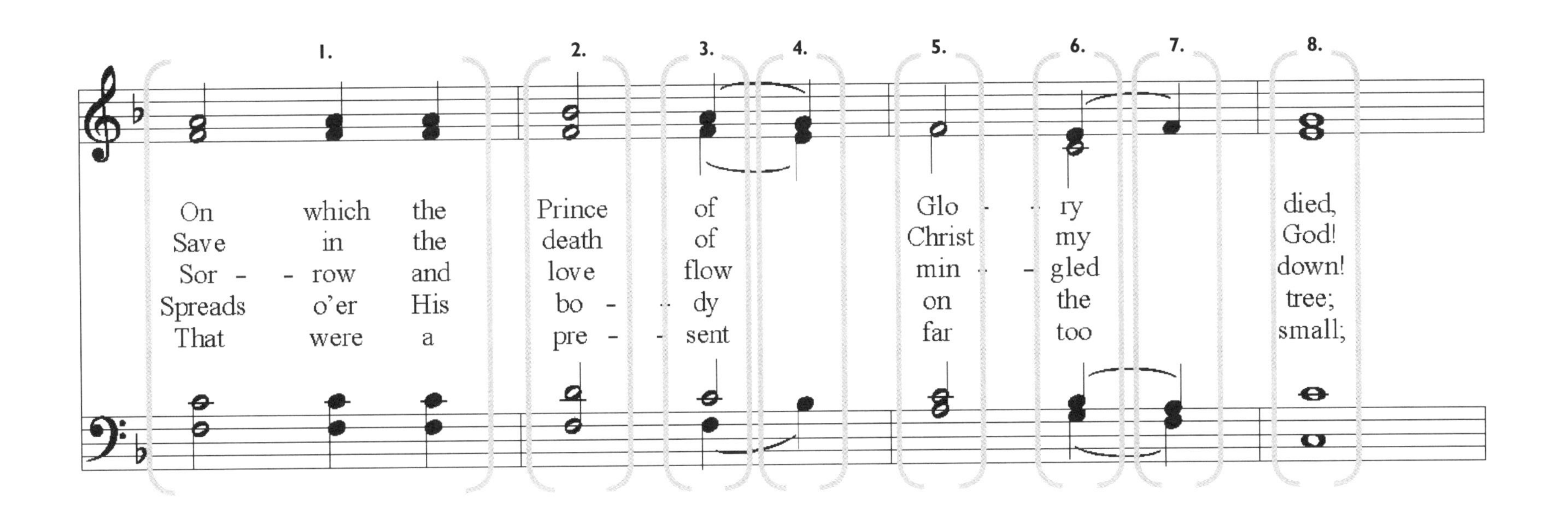

1. I 2. IV^{6}_{4} 3. I

4. $vii^{\circ 6}_{4}$ 5. I^{6} 6. V^{6}_{4} or $vii^{\circ 6}$*

7. I 8. V

**Both answers are correct. For optional teaching, the real answer is a chord called a seventh chord. The notes make up a C major triad with an added B♭ note. The B♭ note is the interval size of a major seventh from the C and therefore the chord is called a C major 7th.*

Exercise 12.8

Use figured bass to analyze the score, an excerpt from "There Is a Fountain Filled with Blood," below.

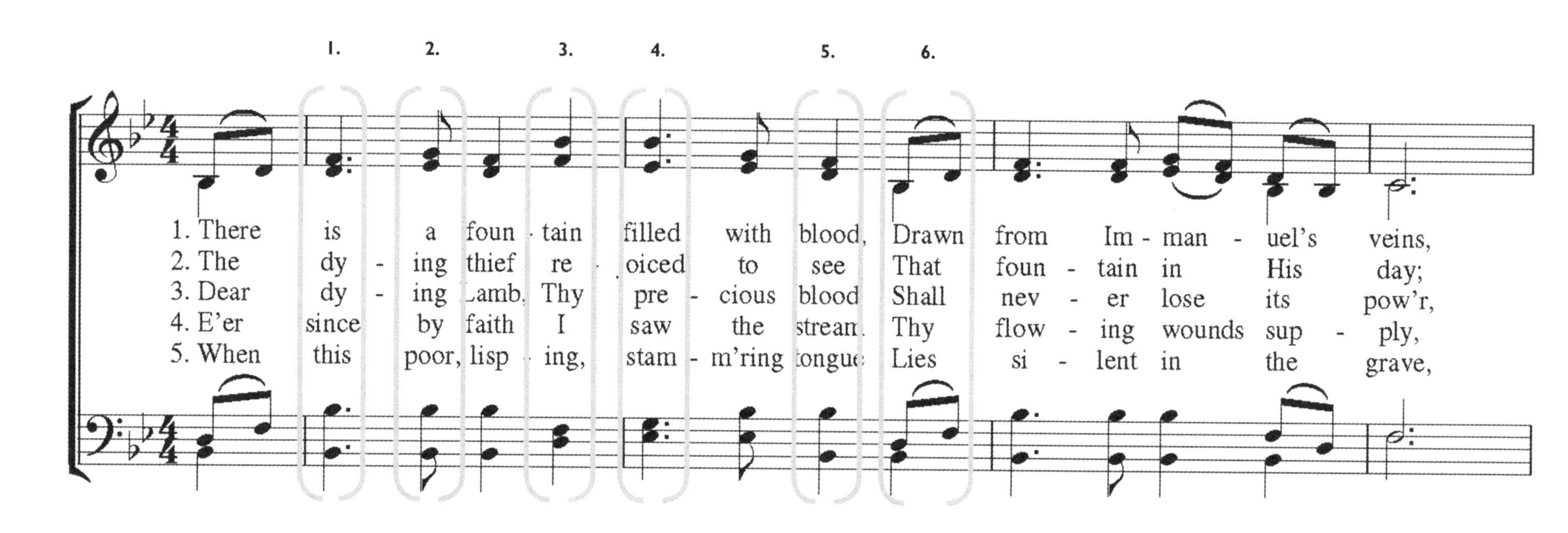

1. I
2. IV^{6}_{4}
3. I^{6}
4. IV
5. I
6. I

13 Review

The Keyboard and Notation

Exercise 13.1 (Chapter 1)

Label the notes on the staves below with the correct note names.

Exercise 13.2 (Chapter 1)

Label the keys on the keyboard using the indicators below.

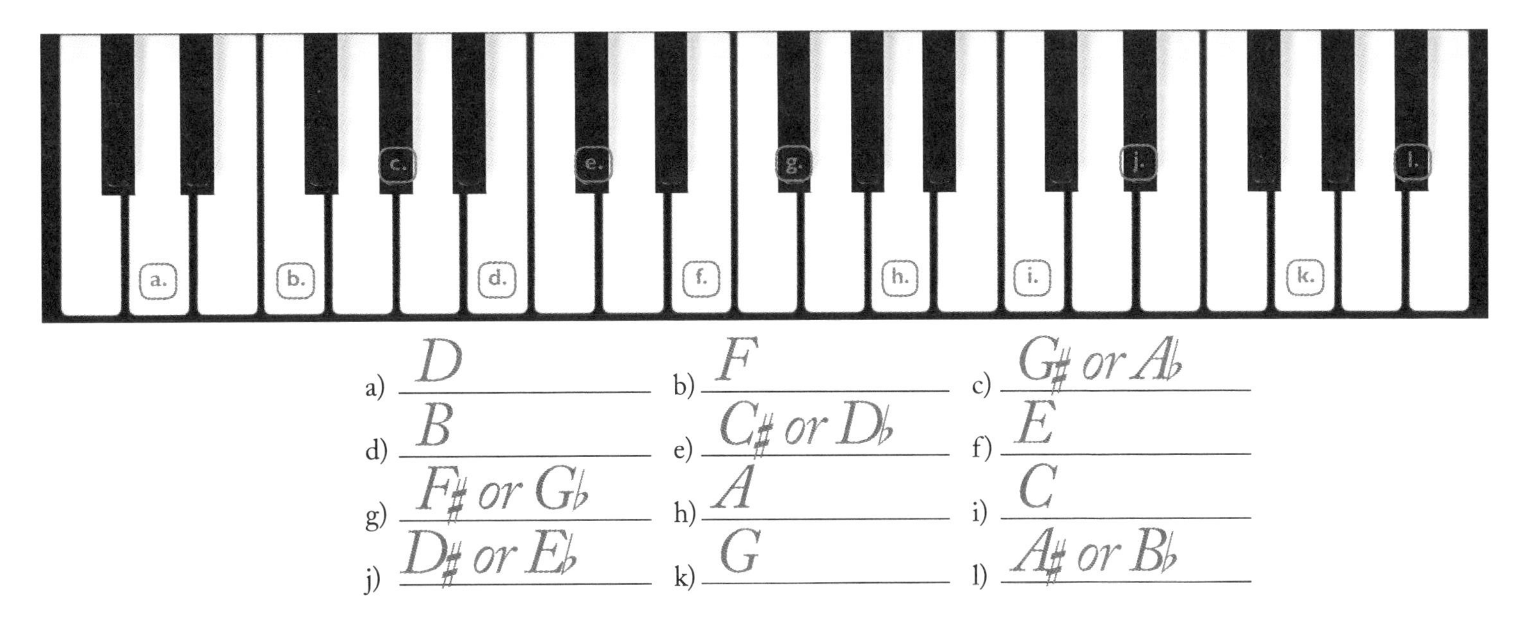

Exercise 13.3 (Chapter 2)

Identify the following symbols.

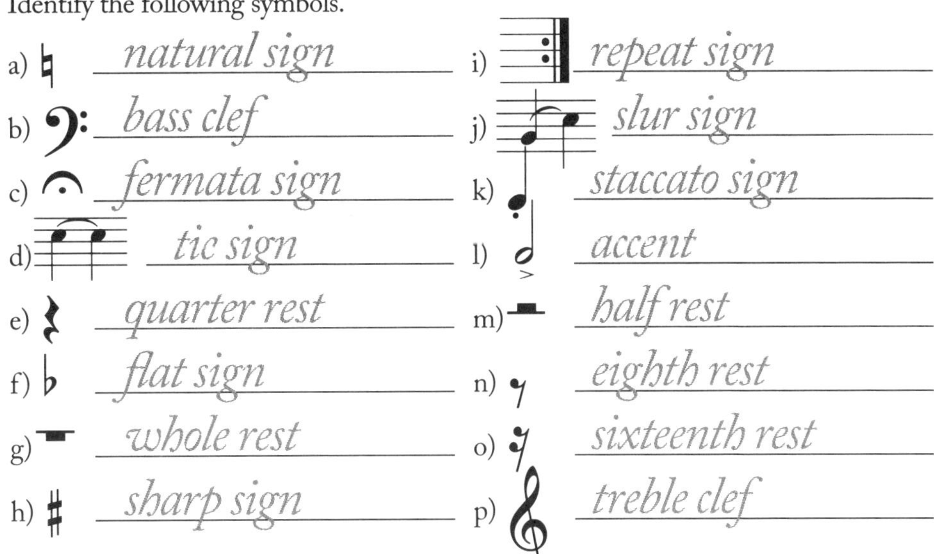

Exercise 13.4 (Chapter 2)

Identify the following note values by name.

a) ♪ *eighth note*

b) 𝅝 *whole note*

c) ♩ *quarter note*

d) 𝅘𝅥𝅯 *sixteenth note*

e) 𝅗𝅥 *half note*

Exercise 13.5 (Chapters 3 and 4)

Match the criteria below with the correct time signature.

a. $\frac{2}{4}$ b. $\frac{3}{8}$ c. $\frac{4}{8}$ d. $\frac{3}{4}$ e. $\frac{3}{2}$ f. $\frac{4}{2}$ g. $\frac{4}{4}$ h. $\frac{2}{2}$ i. $\frac{2}{8}$

h 1. This time signature has two beats per measure with the half note getting the beat.

a 2. This time signature is in duple meter with the quarter note getting the beat.

d 3. This time signature is in triple meter with the quarter note getting the beat.

g 4. This time signature is also known as common meter.

i 5. This time signature has two beats per measure with the eighth note getting the beat.

f 6. This time signature is in quadruple meter with the half note getting the beat.

c 7. This time signature is in quadruple meter with the eighth note getting the beat.

e 8. This time signature has three beats per measure with the half note getting the beat.

b 9. This time signature is in triple meter with the eighth note getting the beat.

Music... will help dissolve your perplexities and purify your character and sensibilities, and in time of care and sorrow, will keep a fountain of joy alive in you.

—Dietrich Bonhoeffer

Exercise 13.6 (Chapters 3 and 4)

Insert bar lines where needed to complete the measures for $\frac{3}{4}$ meter.

Exercise 13.7 (Chapter 5)

Give the whole tone (W) or half tone (H) steps for the scales below. One is a major scale and one is a minor scale.

Exercise 13.8 (Chapter 5)

In each example, the first note of the scale is given; notate the indicated major scale. Use sharps and flats to the left of the note if needed (do not use key signatures).

Exercise 13.9 (Chapter 6)

On the staves below, write the indicated major key signature. Be sure to provide the correct order of sharps or flats within the key signature.

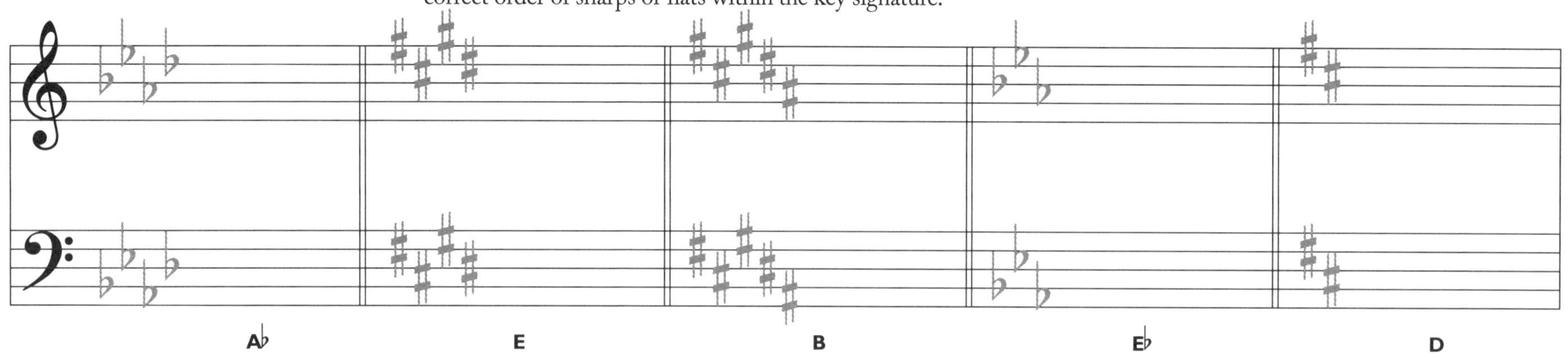

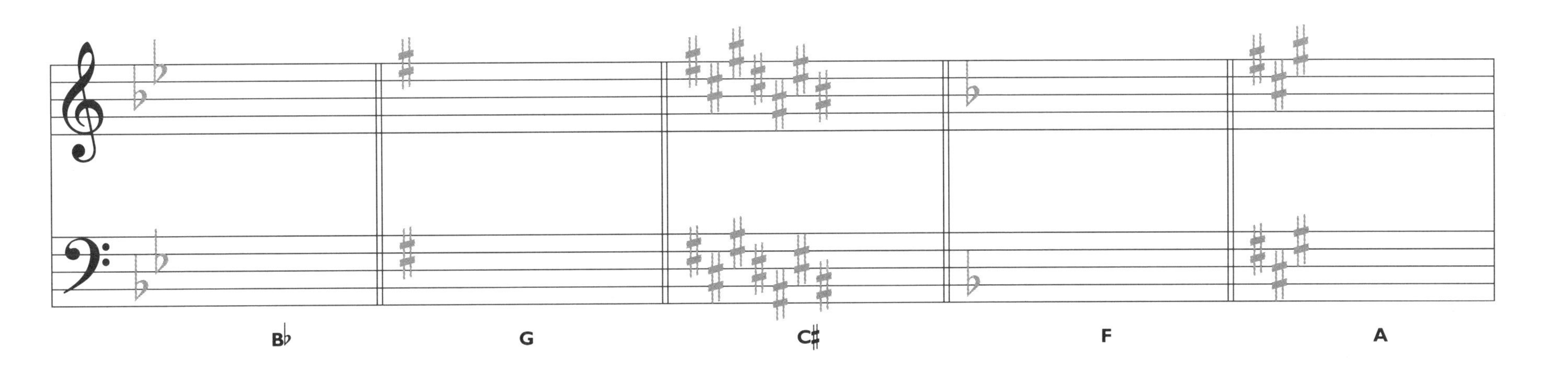

Exercise 13.10 (Chapter 6)

Match the relative keys.

1. __c__ D♯ minor
2. __f__ B major
3. __b__ E major
4. __e__ A major
5. __g__ G minor
6. __d__ D major
7. __a__ A♭ major

a) F minor
b) C♯ minor
c) F♯ major
d) B minor
e) F♯ minor
f) G♯ minor
g) B♭ major

Exercise 13.11 (Chapter 7)

Identify the major key and notate the indicated scale degree names in the following examples.

Exercise 13.12 (Chapter 7)

Use number transposition to transpose the first line of the hymn "When Peace Like a River" into the key of D major. Use bar lines, clef signs, time signatures, and key signatures within your transposition.

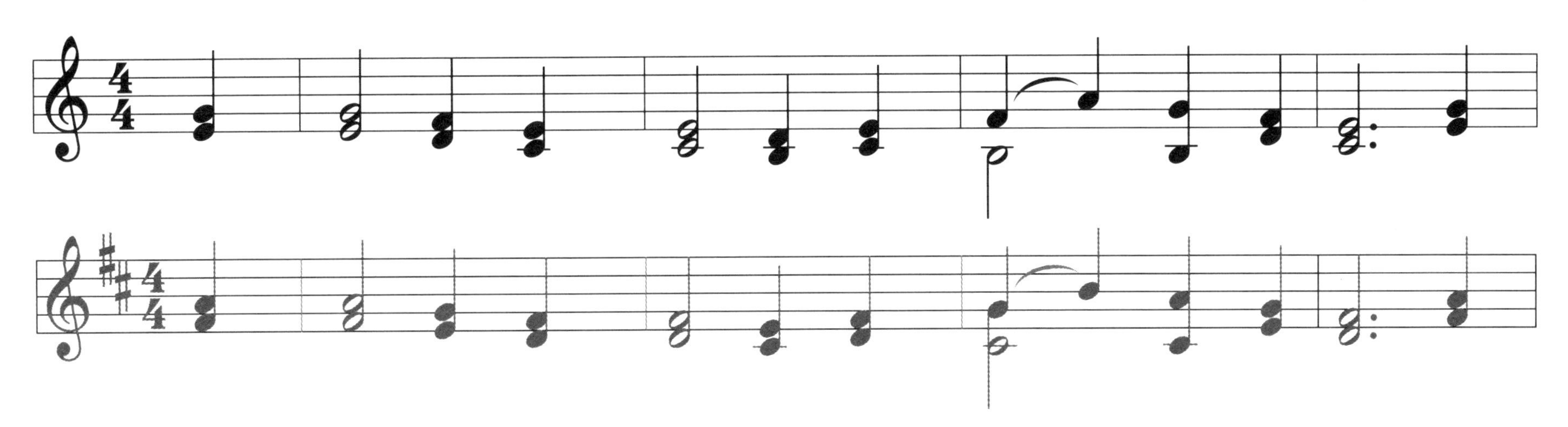

Identify the following harmonic intervals below by quality.

Help: Remember to use the lowest note of the interval as the key signature to determine the quality of interval.

Excerpt from "When Peace Like a River" (Key of C major)

Excerpt from "Be Thou My Vision"

Exercise 13.13 (Chapters 9–12)

Use figured bass to analyze the score below. The lowest note in each group of notes will help you determine the inversion.

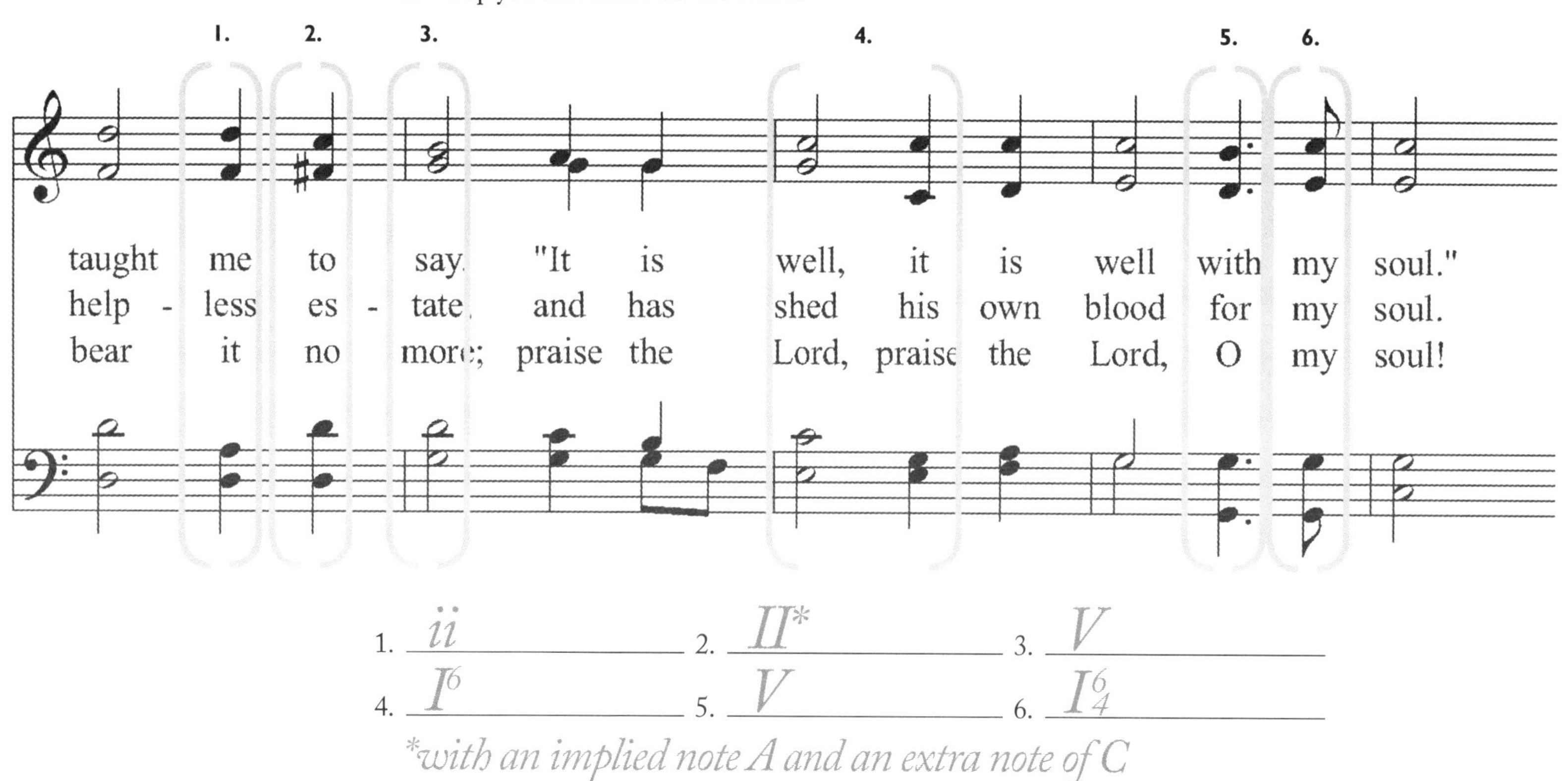

1. *ii*
2. *II**
3. *V*
4. I^6
5. *V*
6. I^6_4

**with an implied note A and an extra note of C*

Bonus Compound Meter

Chapter Review

d 1. Compound meter

 2. Dotted notes

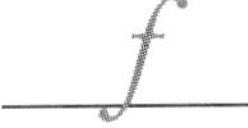 3. Time signature

c 4. Compound triple meter

e 5. Compound quadruple meter

h 6. Top number in compound meter

a 7. Bottom number in compound meter

j 8. Compound duple meter

i 9. Dotted quarter note

b 10. Dotted half note

a) The note value of the divisions of the beat

b) The beat of $\frac{9}{4}$ compound meter

c) Three beats per measure

d) With this meter, the beat is always on a dotted note

e) Four beats per measure

f) Symbol placed immediately after the note to increase the time value by half

g) Only these notes can be divided into three equal parts

h) The number of divisions of the beat in each measure

i). The beat of $\frac{6}{8}$ compound meter

j) Two beats per measure

Daily Exercises for Bonus Chapter

EXERCISES FOR DAY 1

Exercise 1

Read through the bonus chapter and answer the following questions:

1) How many different divisions does the beat have in compound meter? *3*

2) In compound time signatures, what does the top number mean?
Shows how many divisions of the beat there are

3) In compound time signatures, what does the bottom number mean?
The type of note (value) of the divisions of the beat

4) In compound meter, how many beats do duple, triple, and quadruple meter have?
duple = 2, triple = 3, and quadruple = 4

5) Why is compound meter called "compound" meter?
The bottom number in the time signature must be compounded in order to find the beat of the meter.

Exercise 2

Fill in each measure below with notes that correspond to the requested time signature. Be creative with combinations of note values that fit each time signature.

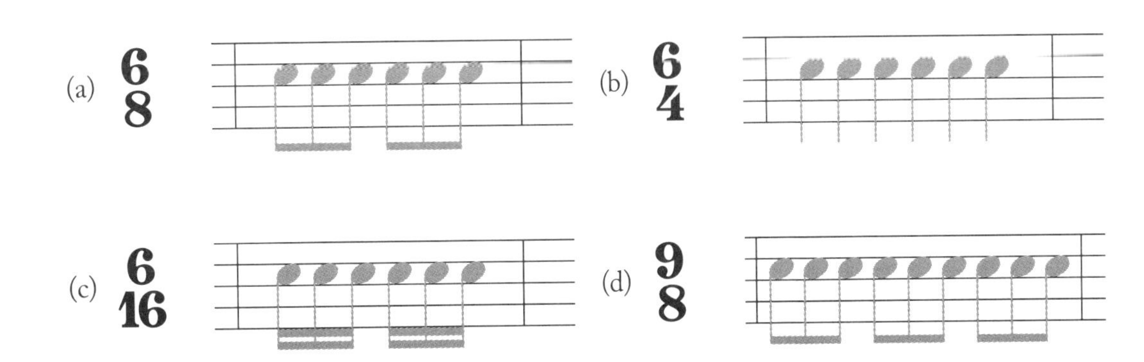

Exercise 3

Write the note value of the beat in each of the following compound time signatures:

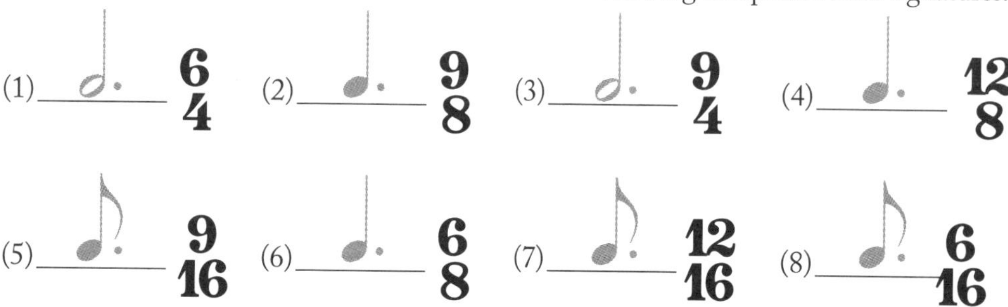

EXERCISES FOR DAY 2

Exercise 4

The following excerpt is the first line from Bach's "Jesu, Joy of Man's Desiring." Use this excerpt to answer the questions below.

1) How many beats are in each measure? 3
2) Which note value is getting the beat?
3) Circle the notation on the treble clef that is played ON the beat in each measure.
4) Circle the notes in the bass clef that are ON the upbeats in each measure.

Exercise 5

Match the simple and compound time signatures with the correct criteria (there may be more than one answer for each time signature).

Answer	Time signature		Criteria
1) cgj	$\frac{4}{4}$		a) Duple meter
2) bjh	$\frac{3}{2}$		b) Triple meter
3) bgke	$\frac{9}{4}$		c) Quadruple meter
4) cik	$\frac{12}{8}$		d) Beat value = ♪.
5) akhe	$\frac{6}{4}$		e) Beat value = 𝅗𝅥.
6) bkg	$\frac{9}{8}$		f) Beat value = ♪
7) bjif	$\frac{3}{8}$		g) Division(s) of beat = ♪
8) ckid	$\frac{12}{16}$		h) Division(s) of beat = ♩
9) akid	$\frac{6}{16}$		i) Division(s) of beat = 𝅘𝅥𝅯
10) ajh	$\frac{2}{2}$		j) Simple meter
			k) Compound meter

Dotted note help

𝅘𝅥𝅯. = 𝅘𝅥𝅰 𝅘𝅥𝅰 𝅘𝅥𝅰

♪. = 𝅘𝅥𝅯 𝅘𝅥𝅯 𝅘𝅥𝅯

♩. = ♪ ♪ ♪

𝅗𝅥. = ♩ ♩ ♩

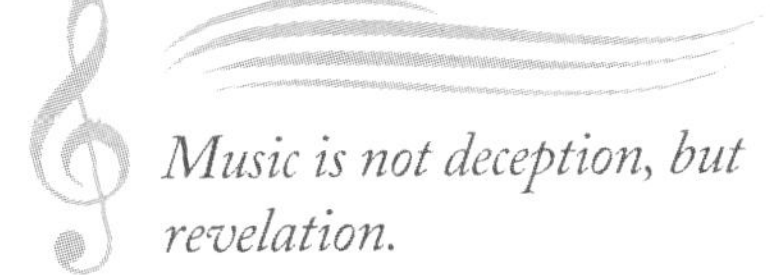

Music is not deception, but revelation.

—Pyotr I. Tchaikovsky

EXERCISES FOR DAY 3

Exercise 6

Re-notate the following rhythm using bar lines to fit the correct time signatures.

Re-notate the following rhythm using bar lines to fit the correct time signatures.

EXERCISES FOR DAY 4

Exercise 7

Match the correct time signature with the melodies below.

a) $\frac{6}{4}$ b) $\frac{9}{8}$ c) $\frac{3}{8}$ d) $\frac{6}{8}$ e) $\frac{4}{4}$

Exercise 8

Use the following measure of notes to answer the questions below:

1. | ♩ ♪ 𝅘𝅥𝅯 𝅘𝅥𝅯 ♪. 𝅘𝅥𝅯 ♩ |

a) Is the rhythm simple or compound meter?

simple

b) Which note value is getting the beat?

quarter note

c) Which note value is the division of the beat?

eighth note

d) What is the time signature of the measure?

4/4

Use the following measure of notes to answer the questions below:

2. | ♩ ♪ ♩. ♪ ♪ ♪ |

a) Is the rhythm simple or compound meter?

compound

b) Which note value is getting the beat?

dotted quarter note

c) Which note value is the division of the beat?

eighth note

d) What is the time signature of the measure?

9/8

Score Analyses

Be Thou My Vision

CONSECRATION

Words: Attr. Dallan Forgaill, 8th Century. Translated by Mary Byrne, 1905 and Eleanor Hull, 1912.
Music: 'Slane' Traditional Irish. Setting: Mark Hamilton Dewey, 2007.

Key Signature: E♭ major
Time Signature: $\frac{3}{4}$ (3 beats per measure with the quarter note getting the beat)
Relative Key Signature: C minor
Intervals labeled below with boxes
Score analysis (figured bass) above
PH = Project Helps, *Math in Motion* appendix

Jn 16:13, Num 12:6

10 10 10 10

Jesu, Joy of Man's Desiring

Johann Sebastian Bach
Classical Conversations Inc. Edition

Key Signature: D major

Time Signature: $\frac{9}{8}$ (3 beats per measure with the dotted quarter note getting the beat)

Relative Key Signature: B minor

Intervals labeled below with boxes

Score analysis (figured bass) above

***PH = Project Helps, *Math in Motion* appendix**

Key Signature: G major
Time Signature: $\frac{4}{4}$ (4 beats per measure with the quarter note getting the beat)
Relative Key Signature: E minor
Intervals labeled below with boxes
Score analysis (figured bass) above

***PH = Project Helps, *Math in Motion* appendix**

Old Hundredth

(From All That Dwells Below the Skies)

This famous tune in the style of a German choral, first appeared in the Geneva Psalter about 1555. The four lines of the Doxology were written by Bishop Thomas Ken (1637-1685). The other set of words given here were written by Isaac Watts (1674-1748), one of the greatest of English hymn writers. This great hymn was conducted with tremendous effect by Patrick S. Gilmore at the great Peace Jubilee in Boson, 1872. (Chorus of 12000, Orchestra 2000), on the arrival of General Grant.

Thos. Ken
Isaac Watts

Louis Bourgeois (?)

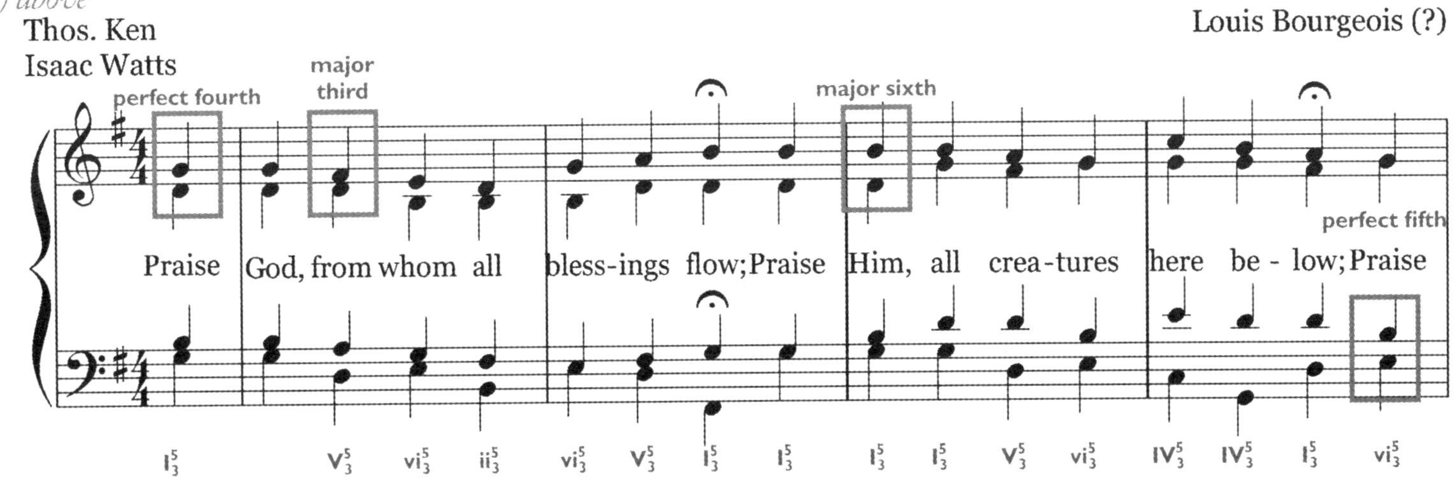

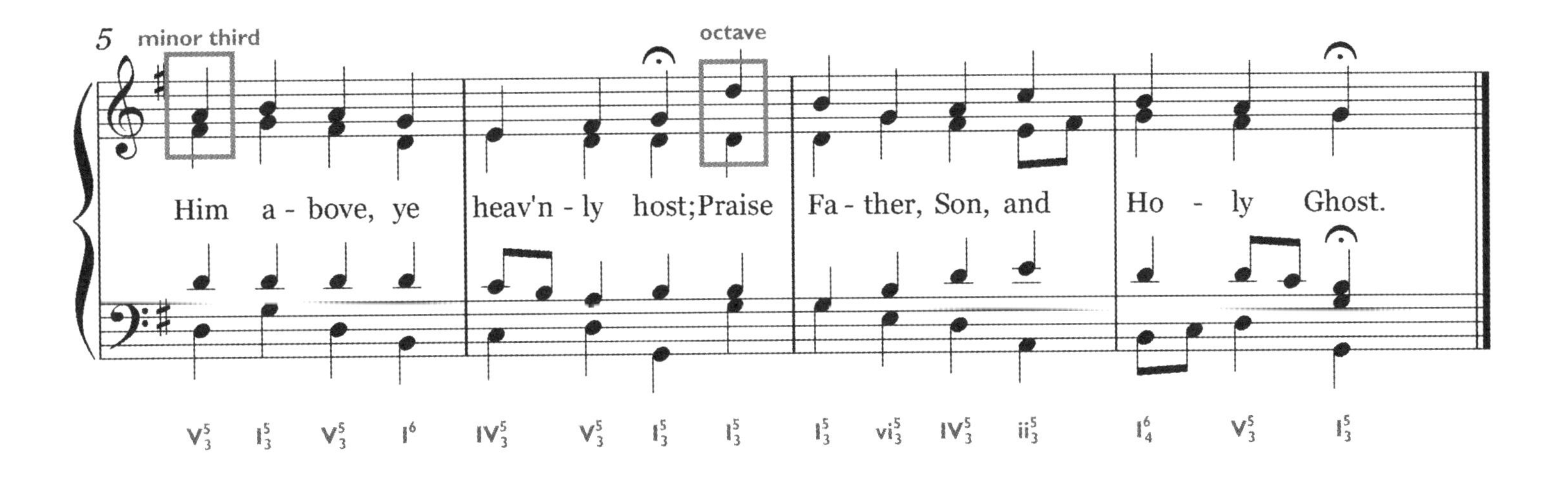

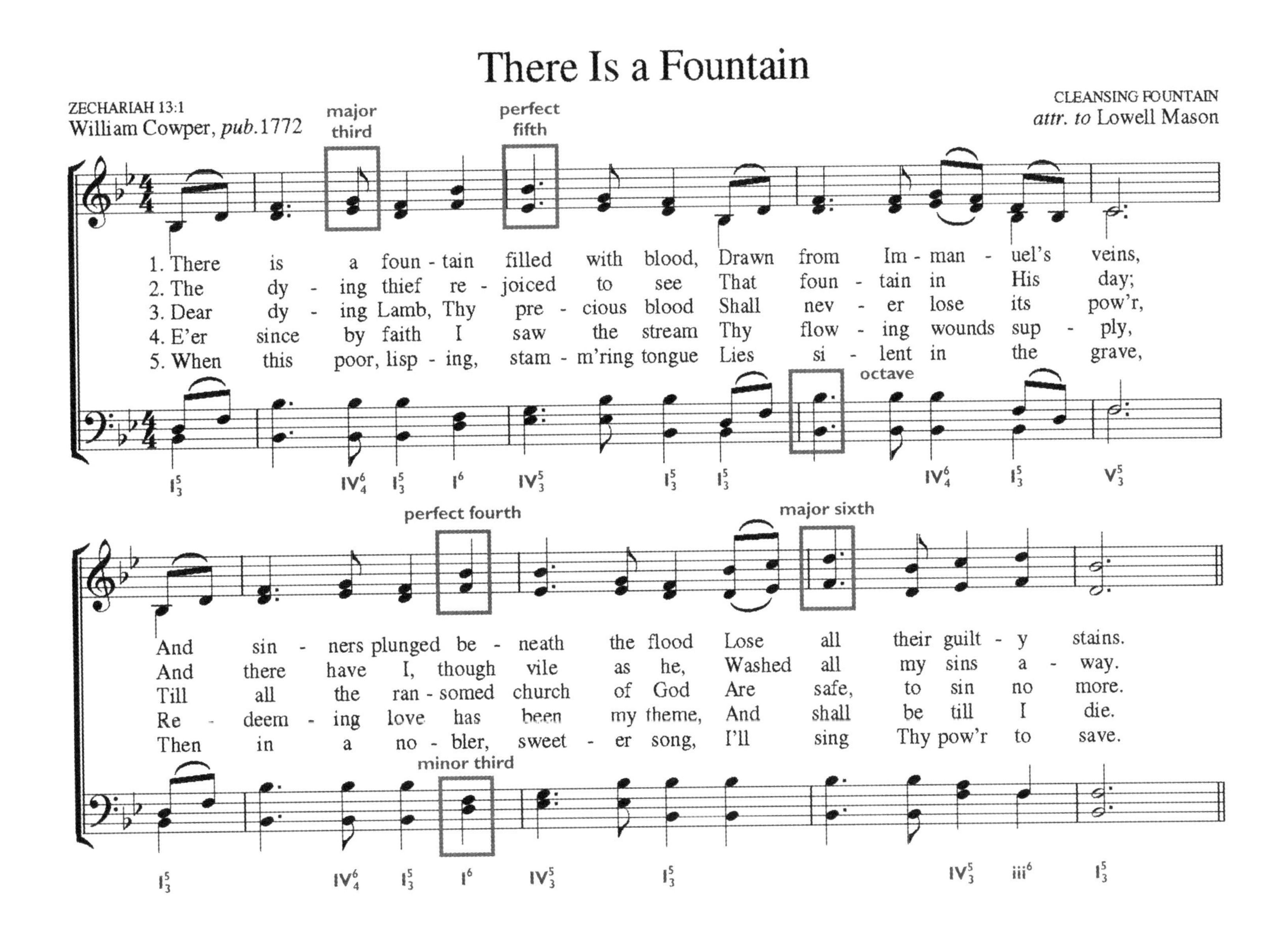
There Is a Fountain
ZECHARIAH 13:1
William Cowper, pub.1772
CLEANSING FOUNTAIN
attr. to Lowell Mason
major third
perfect fifth
1. There is a foun - tain filled with blood, Drawn from Im - man - uel's veins,
2. The dy - ing thief re - joiced to see That foun - tain in His day;
3. Dear dy - ing Lamb, Thy pre - cious blood Shall nev - er lose its pow'r,
4. E'er since by faith I saw the stream Thy flow - ing wounds sup - ply,
5. When this poor, lisp - ing, stam - m'ring tongue Lies si - lent in the grave,
octave
perfect fourth
major sixth
And sin - ners plunged be - neath the flood Lose all their guilt - y stains.
And there have I, though vile as he, Washed all my sins a - way.
Till all the ran - somed church of God Are safe, to sin no more.
Re - deem - ing love has been my theme, And shall be till I die.
Then in a no - bler, sweet - er song, I'll sing Thy pow'r to save.
minor third

Key Signature: B♭ major
Time Signature: $\frac{4}{4}$ (4 beats per measure with the quarter note getting the beat)
Relative Key Signature: G minor
Intervals labeled below with boxes
Score analysis (figured bass) above

***PH = Project Helps, *Math in Motion* appendix**

When I Survey the Wondrous Cross

LENT

Words: Isaac Watts, 1707.
Music: 'Hamburg', Lowell Mason, 1824. Setting: "Northfield Hymnal", 1904.

Key Signature: F major

Time Signature: $\frac{4}{4}$ (4 beats per measure with the quarter note getting the beat)

Relative Key Signature: D minor

Intervals labeled below with boxes

Score analysis (figured bass) above

***PH = Project Helps, *Math in Motion* appendix**

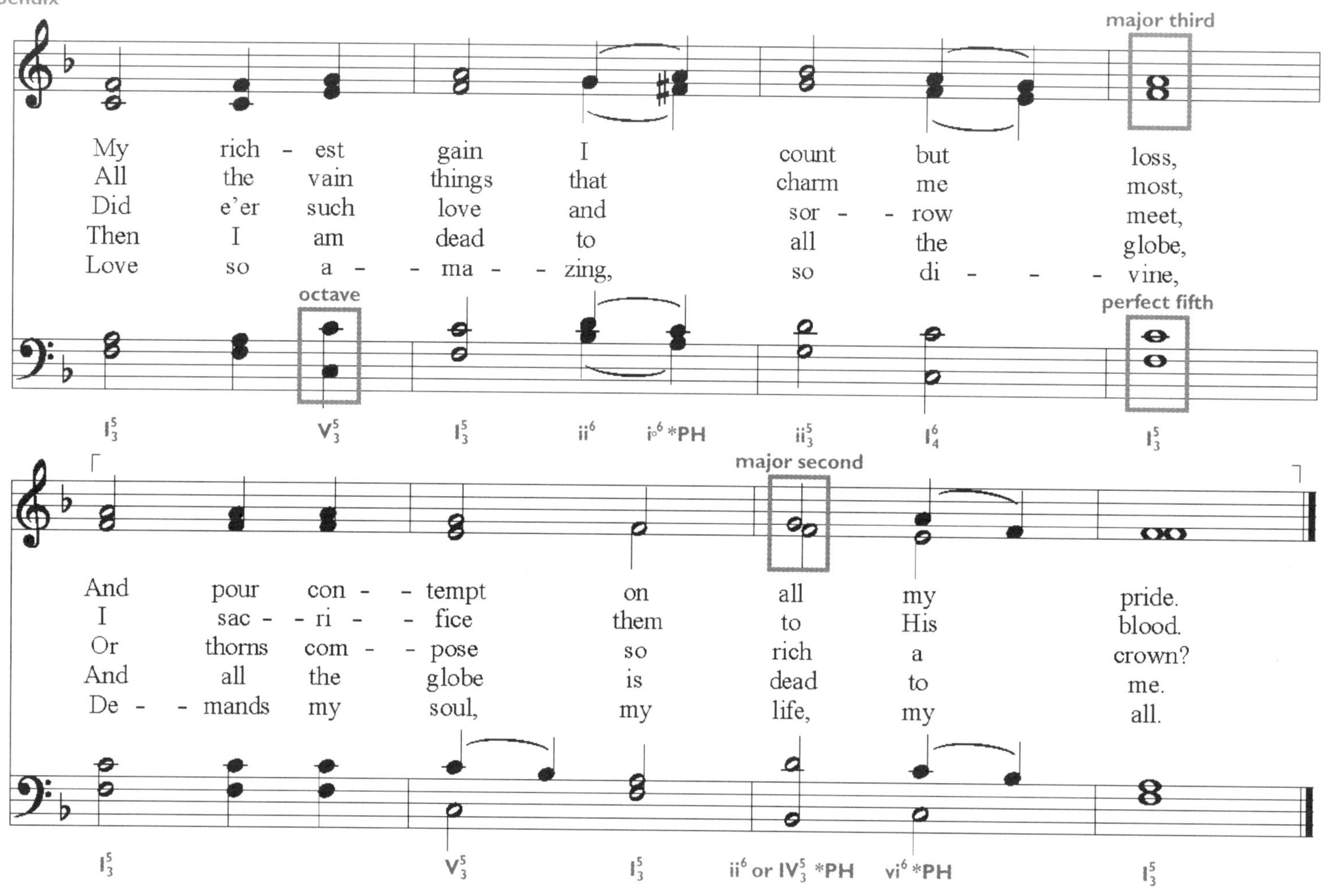

Gal 6:14, Rom 7:24

8888

When Peace Like a River

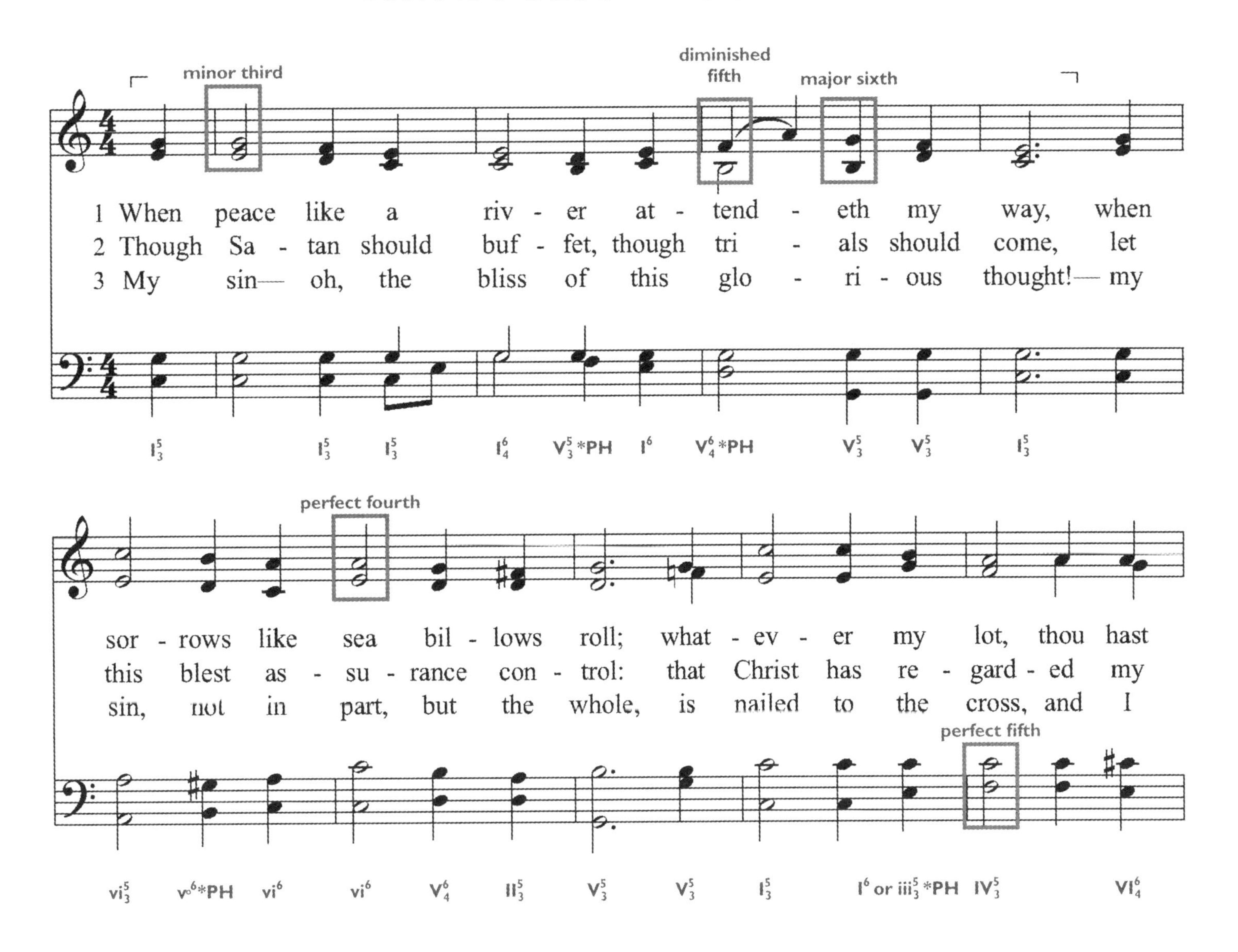

Key Signature: C major

Time Signature: $\frac{4}{4}$ (4 beats per measure with the quarter note getting the beat)

Relative Key Signature: A minor

Intervals labeled below with boxes

Score analysis (figured bass) above

***PH = Project Helps, *Math in Motion* appendix**

major second

taught me to say, "It is well, it is well with my soul."
help - less es - tate, and has shed his own blood for my soul.
bear it no more; praise the Lord, praise the Lord, O my soul!

ii$^5_3$ ii$^5_3$ II$^5_3$ V$^5_3$ vi$^5_3$ *PH V$^5_3$ I^6 I^6 ii^6 or IV$^5_3$ *PH I$^6_4$ V$^5_3$ I$^6_4$ I$^5_3$

Text: Horatio G. Spafford, 1873
Tune: Philip P. Bliss, 1876

11 8 11 9 with refrain
VILLE DU HAVRE
www.hymnary.org/text/when_peace_like_a_river_attendeth_my_way

Refrain (may be sung after final stanza only)
It is well with my soul;
it is well with my soul;
V^5_3 I^5_3 I^6 V^5_3 V^5_3 V^5_3 V^5_3 I^5_3
it is well, it is well with my soul.
I^5_3 I^5_3 IV^5_3 IV^5_3 I^6_4 V^5_3 I^6_4 I^5_3